ISBN 978-1-333-61571-0
PIBN 10526707

1 MONTH OF
FREE
READING

at

www.ForgottenBooks.com

By purchasing this book you are eligible for one month membership to ForgottenBooks.com, giving you unlimited access to our entire collection of over 700,000 titles via our web site and mobile apps.

To claim your free month visit:

www.forgottenbooks.com/free526707

HOW TO WRITE
A POPULAR SONG

By CHARLES K. HARRIS
∴ ∴ Author of "After the Ball" ∴ ∴

PUBLISHED BY
CHARLES K. HARRIS

New York   Chicago   London

Published December 1st, 1906

CONTENTS

Biography   1

Introductory   10

  Chapters

   I.   Lyric Writing   -   -   -   -   11

  II.   The Musical Setting or Melody   18

  III.   The Accompaniment   -   -   26

  IV.   Finishing Touches Previous to Publication   -   46

  ·V.   Printing and Publishing Your Own Composition   49

  VI.   Presenting Manuscript to a Publisher---Selling
Outright---Royalties, Etc.   -   -   -   54

  VII.   Hints and Dont's   -   59

  VIII.   Dictionary of Rhymes   -   -   -   65

1501141

BIOGRAPHY

Charles K. Harris was born at Poughkeepsie, N. Y., on May 1st, 1865. Mr. Harris has been composing songs ever since he was twelve years of age. As a boy he could play almost any instrument and he used to compose songs for special occasions and accompany himself on the banjo. Gradually Mr. Harris drifted into professional song-writing and would compose songs to order for $10.00 and $20.00 a piece, for all sorts of professional people, from the highest to the lowest. Nowadays, Mr. Harris is able to sell his songs and almost estimate their sale even before they are written because his name has become so closely identified with songs of a home-like and simple story character that the public buy a piece of music, with Charles K. Harris as author, often for no other reason than that of the author's name. Mr. Harris is now the head of his great publishing firm and has no partners, being the only composer-publisher in the world who controls his business without the aid of partners. His record is one of long and continued success and should constitute a distinct source of encouragement to every aspiring amateur song-writer. But, to give a better idea of his remarkable success, we will quote Mr. Harris' own words:

"As I am a writer of popular songs, perhaps my career in this field will prove better than any argument I might make that my contention is correct when I state unreservedly that popular song hits are on the increase instead of waning in public appreciation and support. My first two songs which were written for Peter Baker, "Creep, Baby, t'reep," and "Can Hearts So Soon Forget," were placed with A. . Fischer, a publisher in Milwaukee. One thousand copies each were sold, and at that time (fifteen years ago) this w counted a large sale. My next, "Hello Central, Hello," w sung by Charles Horwitz, and about three thousand copi were sold, which in those days was considered very good f a popular ballad. Two more, "Humming Baby to Sleep and "I Wonder," were placed with S. Brainerd & Sons, Cl cago. About one thousand five hundred copies were sold each, and I was supposed to be doing very well.

But what really started the popular song on its meteo career were "After the Ball" and "Kiss and Let's Make U These made the popular song business what it is to-day a presented a new idea to the music-loving public—a comple story, combined with good and catchy music. The id sprang at once into popularity and has been steadily gro ing. At that time the songs then in vogue were founded stories of the sea and so-called high-class ballads of the "The and "Thou" species. These are scarcely heard nowadays.

"After the Ball" lay upon the shelf for over a year, singer caring to take it up on account of its extreme leng It contains three long verses, tells a complete story, and in reality, a condensed drama. After a great deal of hustlin hard work and persistent effort, a copy of it reached Miss M Irwin, and, being introduced by her on Broadway, create sensation. It was then introduced in Milwaukee by Jan Aldrich Libbey, in Hoyt's "A Trip to Chinatown" Compa and on the Coast by Dick Jose, while Helen Mora sang it the leading vaudeville houses throughout the country. Tl proved the first popular song educator. This was followed "Kiss and Let's Make Up," another story song, which a scored heavily. Still the old-time publishers continued frown upon the popular songs, calling them trash and insisting that there would be no demand for such rubbish when "After the Ball" died out. But they were behind the times as "Kiss and Let's Make Up" proved that the public wanted a song with a story—a story with a moral.

The next difficulty that confronted me was to get new topics for songs. It was claimed that there would not be topics enough which would prove acceptable, but I kept close watch on the current events of the day. Being an inveterate theatre-goer, I received many suggestions from the stage. For example, about ten years ago such plays as "The Second Mrs. Tanqueray" and "The Crust of Society" were in vogue. I then wrote "Cast Aside," "Fallen by the Wayside" and "There'll Come a Time Some Day." The public snapped at them. Over 300,000 copies were printed of each of these songs, amounting to almost one million copies. Then came an era of society dramas, such as Belasco's "Charity Ball" and "The Wife." I wrote and published at that time "While the Dance Goes On," "Hearts," "You'll Never Know," and "Can Hearts So Soon Forget," which sold enormously.

Despite these successes the old fogy publishers and music trade buyers were still skeptical and would only purchase in quantities to fill absolute orders. They would not advertise my songs nor announce them in their catalogues or advertisements, leaving it entirely to the composer to create a demand for his compositions.

During the J. K. Emmet, W. J. Scanlon and Gus Williams epoch I wrote "Humming Baby to Sleep," "Creep, Baby, Creep," and "School Bells," differing entirely from those heretofore mentioned. Then came Bronson Howard's "Shenandoah," Gillette's "Held by the Enemy," "Secret Service,"

., showing military dramas to be the vogue. I composed two soldier songs, "Just Tell Her That I Loved Her Too" and "Break the News to Mother," both proving enormous hits and putting the popular song a notch higher in the estimation of both the music trade and the music-loving public.

Eventually Zangwill's "Children of the Ghetto" and Jacob Litt's productions of "The Ghetto" and "Zora" held the boards. It was then I wrote the song story, "A Rabbi's Daughter," which also had a large sale. Contemporaneously with the pastoral dramas like "Way Down East," "Shore Acres," etc., I wrote "Mid the Greenfields of Virginia" and "In the Hills of Old Carolina."

After these there came a craze for ragtime, and it looked as though the descriptive love story and child songs would be forever discarded. The Williams and Walker "Black Patti" and other colored organizations were the rage for a time, all of them featuring ragtime music. Not to be outdone, I wrote "Ma Black Tulip" and "Don't Forget to Tell Me That You Love Me Honey," both successes.

Eventually the public became satiated with ragtime and I cast about for a new theme, having covered the ground pretty thoroughly for so many years.

Just then Julia Marlowe scored in "When Knighthood Was in Flower," a drama with heart interest. I promptly brought forth "I've a Longing in My Heart for You, Louise," and "I'm Wearing My Heart Away For You." The sale of those two songs reached over one million copies.

A few years ago I witnessed a performance of one of Theodore Kremer's melodramas, the principal character in it being a child. "The Little Princess" was announced for production here and I presented for public approval the now celebrated child song, "Hello Central, Give Me Heaven," following it (at the earnest solicitation of the trade) with another entitled, "Always in the Way," the sales of which, I think, will equal the enormous figures attained by "After the Ball" I then gave to the now expectant public "For Sale, A Baby," another enormous hit. The idea for this song was suggested to me by a story in the daily papers, detailing the agony of an unfortunate woman who offered her child for sale because she was unable to care for it So great has the demand become for my works that 50,000 copies were bespoken for another child song, "Why Don't They Play With Me

It is the composers who originate who win fame. Many song-writers think they can score by copying another idea that is on the market, either in title or music Occasionally they come near it, but as a rule the public has no sympathy with imitators and the name of a well-known composer on an imitation is likely to act as a boomerang Originality always pays. The easiest way for a composer of music or a lyric writer to keep up to date is to watch the trend of events in the daily papers

Another—and very important—reason why popular songs are in greater demand to-day than heretofore lies in the fact that only a few years ago a person who was the proud owner of a piano was looked upon as the possessor of wealth. In these days every workingman who has a family owns a piano, an organ, banjo, guitar or mandolin, and frequently several instruments may be found in a single family. Of course, this creates a demand for the lighter class of popular music.

Then again, the public schools all teach the rudiments of music, free scholarships in conservatories have been established, which induces a large number of young folks to compete. In fact, it is almost as much a part of a child's education as learning to read and write. I might go even **further** and' say that every girl in the United States whose parents can possibly afford it is to-day receiving music lessons.

A large demand for popular songs is also created by the phonographs, graphophones, pianolas and automatic instruments of all kinds.

It must also be remembered that until a **few years ago** there was no such thing as a vaudeville show, **merely a few** variety houses, patronized by men only. As there were no women and children in the audience, popular ballads could not be heard by those who now purchase them. Minstrel shows were the only performances where a ballad was sung. This has all been changed. At least one vaudeville theatre has been established in every city of any size in the United States. If the audience hears a song that strikes its fancy, the local dealer is promptly besieged with orders. The vaudeville houses to-day present the best singers that the market affords, where only a few years ago a high-class singer on the variety stage was unknown.

The final prejudices against the popular ballad by high-class singers were overcome when Mme. Adelina Patti introduced and sang in America on her farewell tour a song written by me, especially for the occasion, entitled "The Last Farewell." That broke down all barriers, and to-day any high-class performer in the world will gladly sing a popular ballad.

The illustration of songs has also helped to make them popular. Having the scenes and characters of a song thrown upon a canvas during its rendition has proved a great hit in every city where it has been introduced, and, as all my songs readily lend themselves to illustration, it has aided in popularizing them. I have sent photographers to such distan points as California, Texas, Alaska, and even the Philippines, wherever a scene is laid, to secure original photographs taken on the spot. A set of negatives frequently costs as much as $1,500. But the public wants the best and shows its appreciation when it receives it. The sale of songs shows that the American public appreciates originality in song composition as in everything else.

Only a few years ago a sheet music counter in a department store was unheard of. To-day in the largest dry goods emporiums and department stores in New York, down to the smallest in every city in the United States, can be found a music counter where all the popular songs of the day are on sale.

Musical comedy, which has been the rage for the past few years, has also been instrumental in creating and increasing the sale of popular songs, as a musical comedy is made up almost entirely of popular music."

It may also be interesting to the readers of this book to glance over the remarkable list of popular song hits written and composed, both words and music, by Mr. Harris. Each and every song on the list has sold over one hundred thousand copies, while some have sold as high as one million and a half:

"All for the Love of a Girl," "After the Ball," "After Nine," "A Rabbi's Daughter," "Always in the Way," "Break the News to Mother," "Better Than Gold," "Before and After Taken," "Cast Aside," "Creep, Baby, Creep," "Can Hearts So Soon Forget," "Dear College Chums," "Don't Forget to Tell Me That You Loves Me Honey," "Do You Think You Could Learn to Love Me," "Down in the Vale of Shenandoah," "Dreaming Love of You," "Fallen by the Wayside," "Fifty Years Ago," "For Old Times' Sake," "Farewell, Sweetheart May," "For Sale, A Baby," "Fly Away Birdie to Heaven,"

"Hearts," "Humming Baby to Sleep," "Hello, Cenſra
Hello," "Hello Central, Give Me Heaven," "I've Just Com
Back to Say Good-bye," "I've Been Faithful to You," "I Loɪ
Her Just the Same," "Is Life Worth Living," "I Love You i
Spite of All," "I Was Talking in My Sleep," "I Wonder,
Wonder," "I Heard Her Voice Again," "I Used to Know Hɛ
Years Ago," "I've a Longing in My Heart for You, Louise,
"In the Hills of Old Carolina," "I'm Wearing My Heaɪ
Away for You," "In Dear Old Fairyland," "In the Good Oɪ
Fashioned Way," "I'm Trying So Hard to Forget You,
"Just Behind the Times," "Just Tell Her That I Loved Hɛ
Too," "Just One Kiss," "Just Next Door," "Just A Gleam ɑ
Heaven in Her Eyes," "Kiss and Let's Make Up," "Leoni
Queen of My Heart," "Little Sweetheart," "Last Night as th
Moon was Shining, "Love and Kisses" (Caprice), "Ma Fiɪ
pino Babe," "Mid the Greenfields of Virginia," "Ma Blac
Tulip," "Must We Say Good-bye Forever, Nellie Dear,
"Only a Tangle of Golden Curls," "One Night in June," "O
the Sands at Night," "Sitting by the Kitchen Door,
"Strangers," "Since Katie Rides a Wheel," "School Bells,
"Sweet Maid Divine," "There is No Flag Like the Red, Whiɪ
and Blue," "The Organgrinder's Serenade," "There'll Con
a Time," "Then Comes the Sad Awakening," "Too Latɛ
Alas, Too Late!" "Tis Not Always Bullets that Kill," "Tl
Tie That Binds," "The Last Farewell" (Adelina Patti's Far
well Song), "The Girls of My Dreams," "Will I Find M
Mamma There," "While the Dance Goes On," "When tl
Lights Went Out," "Which Shall It Be," "Waiting for Foo
steps That Never Came," "What Does the Flower Say," "M
Heart is Weary Just for You," "Linda, Can't You Love Yoɪ
Joe," "Suppose I'd Meet You Face to Face," "Through tl
Old Farm Gate," "Nobody Knows, Nobody Cares," "Only

Hord You in My Arms Again," "I Do Not Blame You Darling," "And a Little Child Shall Lead Them," "Belle of the Ball," etc.

Page upon page might be written setting forth facts as to why the popular song is growing in public favor and will always grow as long as there are musical instruments and stages to exploit it and as long as the world produces composers with originality.

INTRODUCTORY.

In presenting this book to the amateur song **writers an** composers of America the aim has been to treat **the variou** subjects and chapters in a form that is comprehensible an easily understood by all. Technical and foreign terms hav been avoided as far as possible, and wherever it has been n cessary to make use of them an explanation in plain Englis follows.

It must **also be** clearly understood that there is no inte tion of conveying the impression that in this short treati on the subject of popular song-writing will be found an secret formula for the creation of talent and genius in th particular line of work. Talent and genius, often latent j some persons, are never acquired. They are the gifts Nature, and unless she has bestowed them in greater or le degree upon the individual, the purpose of this book in see ing to open the way and make the path clear, will avail not ing. The remarks, rules and suggestions offered herein a the fruits of many years of practical experience, and a those which have been closely observed by all the great sor writers and composers.

The word "popular," as used in this treatise in referen to songs, has been employed to expressly designate the vario classes of songs which are written, published and sun whistled and hummed by the great American "unmusica public, as distinguished from the more highly cultivat musical class which often decries and scoffs at the tantalizin and ear-haunting melodies that are heard from ocean ocean in every shape and form. Argument in favor of the merit is undoubtedly proven beyond question by their eno mous sale; and many a sad and weary heart has been mad glad by the strains of these "popular" songs.

CHAPTER I.

LYRIC-WRITING.

Different Styles of Songs.

To the ambitious amateur writer of song lyrics, more especially those that come under the head of "popular" songs, naturally arises the question, "What kind of a song shall I write to achieve fame and success?" First of all, it is necessary that the writer acquaint himself with the various style or styles of song that happen to be in vogue. This, of course, can easily be ascertained, either by following the performances at the theatres, or by carefully noting the display of music at the stores. It is practically useless, of course, to write in a style or on a subject which has already run the gamut of "popular" demand. For instance, the day of the rough Coon song, the Indian song, and several others, is temporarily over; and no matter how well written a song on such subjects as these may be, it will not "take" or be accepted by the public. Styles in songs change as quickly as those in ladies' millinery. Each seems to have a cycle which comes and goes, and whose length of life is only increased occasionally by the introduction of some new idea which is merely wedged into the original style, or mode. One season Coon songs may be all the rage, then suddenly the simple love ballad sets the pace, only to give way in turn to something else that hits the fancy of a public that is always capricious in these matters, whatever it may be in others.

Some sudden National, or big public disturbance or sensation, will bring about a demand and create an interest in certain styles of song, where new ideas, or more often old ideas made to look like new, are worked in and adapted to the special occasion or circumstances that are for the moment engrossing public attention Thus, for instance, the outbreak of war is always followed by the publication of every conceivable kind of "war song," of which "Just Break the News to Mother" was a recent and notable example.

The late war between Russia and Japan aroused interest in Japanese songs, not necessarily treating on war themes, but Japanese in subject and atmosphere. When the great battleship, "The Maine," was destroyed, two songs, written around this tragedy, namely, "'Tis not Always Bullets That Kill" and "Just tell Her That I Loved Her Too," achieved great success. The St Louis Fair gave birth to numberless songs having reference to "The Pike"; and new fashions and customs, as well as a thousand other incidents and causes, could be mentioned as having been responsible for certain styles in songs

Songs, however, are usually classified by the writers, publishers, and trade, under the following principal heads:

a.—The Home, or Mother Song.

b.—The Descriptive, or Sensational Story Ballad.

c.—The popular Waltz Song. (On a thousand and one subjects.)

d.—The Coon Song. (Rough, Comic, Refined, Love or Serenade, etc.)

e.—The March Song. (Patriotic, War, Girl, Character, etc.)

f.—The Comic Song. (Topical, Character, Dialect, etc.)

g.—The Production Song (for Interpolation in big Musical Productions, entailing the use of a Chorus of Men, or Girls, or both, and certain novel action, costume, or business.)

h.—The Popular Love Ballad.

j.—High Class Ballads.

k.—Sacred Songs.

There are, of course, many subdivisions and classifications about which it is not necessary to enter into detail, however, as each of the above heads will be treated separately in another chapter.

The lyric writer should bear in mind that originality, conciseness, good metre and rhythm, and above all, good grammar, are the main essentials required. If the song be Character, Dialect, or otherwise, the lyric writer should be careful to keep in the atmosphere of the subject, to seek strong points and good wit wherever applicable. If you cannot write lyrics for a certain style of song, *don't attempt it.* "Every man to his last" is a very wise and practical axiom for lyric or melody writers of popular songs.

Choice of good singable words in the writing of lyrics is also vital. Words with harsh consonants, many syllabled words, words or phrases that do not seem to speak or sing smoothly, should be studiously discarded. Tell your tale tersely, make it as strong as possible, and let it almost sing itself as you recite it.

In most song lyrics, excepting those for topical, or comic songs, two verses are ample. One argument in favor of this is, that the public singer of your songs, who is, of course, its best advertisement, rarely cares to use more than two verses. If three are written, and the third verse contains, as it naturally would, the climax, or moral of your story, the public seldom hears it sung, and accordingly entertains a totally wrong impression as to the merits of your composition, which to them appears unfinished, and, therefore, uninteresting. Thus, a handicap is attached to the song at the outset.

A very important point is the construction of the Refrai or Chorus, of the song. Upon this part of the compositi rests, in a majority of instances, the ultimate success or fa ure of a song. Wherever possible, it is a very wise plan write your chorus words so that they are equally applicab to every verse. There are exceptions to this, of course, b it is well to apply this rule pretty generally, as the publ readily retains the words of the one refrain, whereas tv different sets often retard popularity. In Comic, or Topic songs, the two or three lines preceding the last one are fi quently varied, as they contain the "laugh" or "gag" line in other words, the strong point of the verse is here reveale The last line in the chorus, or refrain, is very rarely change as nearly all songs that come under the head of "Popula depend on this line for their title. To put it shortly, get good line for the finish of your chorus, and your successf title is assured. It is hardly necessary to add that a real good title is almost everything, though to find one is almo as difficult as the naming of the first baby. It is most e sential that the public get their attention fixed on this line the outset. In this way they retain it in their mind ai know what to ask for in purchasing.

Not so many years ago, refrains to songs were not co sidered so important, but now the chorus is looked upon the kernel of the whole song. In ninety-nine cases out every hundred it is the words of the refrain and the melo that the public sings, whistles and hums, and so it becom known as "the popular hit."

Alliteration is often very effective in song lyrics. O excerpt from a well-known verse is here quoted to show t cleverness of this trick:

"Linger longer Lucy, linger longer Lou."

Clever catchy lines, or phrases, are always to be looked for. In sprightly, comic, or even popular songs with a love story, if well used, they often help to make a song. Two fine examples of the use of "catch lines" in this way are here given:

I.   From "Just One Girl."

"There are only two flies in the honey."

II.   From "Bedelia."

"I'll be your Chauncey Olcott if you'll be my Molly O."

These two lines were caught up more quickly by the public and attracted more attention almost than anything else in the two songs. There are, of course, many other equally well-known cases where the "catch line" practically made the song.

A euphonious title is a great essential to the making of a successful song. Let it be pleasant equally to the eye and ear. The shorter and more concise it is, the better. In one, two, or three, or half a dozen words (more, if absolutely necessary) it should indicate the story, just as in a newspaper article the head line conveys the whole idea, if cleverly written, of what follows.

Avoid slang, or *double entente* lines and phrases. They may seem witty and clever, but they ruin the chances for the song to sell well. Refined people do not care to have songs containing such words or allusions seen in their homes, or used by members of their family.

Always look to the selling qualities of a song. Principal among these are, an original idea. a catchy title, a haunting melody, clean words, good grammar (whether for ballads or comic songs), conciseness, strong points, and last but not

least, a good publisher. Advice on this point will be offere
in another chapter.

When your first verse is written, and you start on tl
next, always be careful that the accented words, or syllabl
correspond exactly, line by line, with those in the openin
verse, and thus fit the accented notes of your melody. S
that the "feet" in each metre are numerically the same i
each verse. The temptation to crowd in extra syllables c
words in succeeding verses must be rigorously resiste
There is no exception to this rule.

It is also highly advisable, and often imperative, that
single syllable or monosyllable correspond to each note c
the melody.

EXAMPLES.

(GOOD)

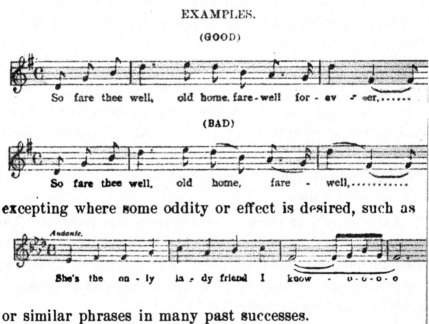

excepting where some oddity or effect is desired, such as

or similar phrases in many past successes.

Short verses and refrains are now found to bring the be
results. A few years ago the verses were twice the lengt
they now are. To-day, they are regarded as tedious and ol

fashioned. The idea is to get into the chorus, or refrain, as quickly as possible, thus telling a good story in as few words as you can, which, as we all know, is the keynote of success in story-telling, and applies equally well in song-writing.

CHAPTER II.

THE MUSICAL SETTING OR MELODY.

The lyrics of your song being written and revised so tha
their final form presents little or no room for improvemen
apparently, the next consideration is the melody, and, afte
that, the accompaniment. Of course, it often happens tha
the writer is equally capable of composing his own musi
thereto; and where this is the case, matters are naturally con
siderably simplified. The results achieved by writers wh
are the creators of both the words and the melody, are, o
should be, obviously better, than where the work is split uj
between two parties. Nevertheless, it must not be suppose
that two heads in this business are not very often better tha
one.

In recent years, many of the most successful popular song
as far as the music was concerned, have been composed b
individuals who merely possessed a natural ability for orig
nating effective melody. In very many instances, indeed
these "composers" were unable to read a note of music, o
even to pick out their melodies on any instrument. Unde
these circumstances they simply hummed or whistled thei
tune to some other party who was sufficiently gifted to trans
fer same to paper. Others, again, could pick out their me
ody, say, on a piano, and get the notes down on paper in mor
or less coherent form. After this, of course, much remaine
still to be done, the principal item being the provision an
arrangement of the best possible and most effective form c
accompaniment.

Writers of lyrics often, unconsciously, construct thei

lines to the rhythm of some more or less tangible melody that exists in their minds, without their being able to actually materialize it. It is therefore advisable, when presenting your lyrics to a composer of music, to either hum the words to your melody—or rather, the *swing* of what would be your melody if properly developed—or recite them just in the way they would be sung. By this means the composer is enabled to readily grasp your own idea of the proper lilt and rhythm of your verse. In quite a number of cases, a set of words is capable of being read in half a dozen different ways, so far as regards their "swing." In others, to the composer, they seem to have no rhythmic swing at all, until their originator comes along and solves the little puzzle. Composers should take heed of this, because any sign of halting in a melody makes the song at once seem unnatural or unfinished, and it suffers accordingly. To show how easy it sometimes is to find different methods of setting the music to a set of words, one has only to recall the example once given by the famous composer, Sir Arthur Sullivan. Every one knows that for lyric-writing Mr. W. S. Gilbert, his collaborator, has never yet been equalled. Yet, when the latter wrote the lyric, "Were I Thy Bride," from the opera, "The Yeomen of the Guard," Sir Arthur showed he could have composed music to it in no less than eight entirely different styles of rhythm. Mr. Gilbert only had one in his mind; the composer found eight, all of them equally good.

The advantages of mutual consultation and help between the composer and writer of words are many, but that just referred to is the most important.

When authors discover composers or composers unearth authors who prove clever and successful, it is as well that they form a "team," or partnership, and write exclusively together, where possible. Constant interest in each other's work develops sympathy between them, a sort of telepathic tie is formed, and they grasp each other's undeveloped, or finished ideas instantaneously. They grow familiar with each other's style and individuality, which results in a completed work that is in harmony with itself, and, consequently, good in all points. The melody and words of a song must be in harmony. A skillful composer will nearly always make the melody speak the words and reflect the sentiment and atmosphere of the lyrics.

Quite frequently a composer will complete a beautiful or catchy melody, irrespective of any lyrics, but in these cases the composer can and does readily suggest the style, sentiment, and even the title of the song he desires to evolve from this "song without words." He feels the style and sentiment; the very notes of the melody seem to speak the story in a more or less vague fashion.

A famous playwright in New York City once made the remark, in speaking of his work: "I sometimes sit and think for days and my mind seems hopelessly blank. Suddenly a vague but indefinite idea appears. It seems to be a long way off, but as I think and think it comes closer, until gradually it develops from a misty embryo into a well defined shape or form, upon which I work until the beautifully finished production is an actuality." So it is with the author or composer of songs, especially writers of novelties. A misty, vague, indefinite idea appears, from which new thoughts and ideas rapidly spring, till, finally, the original novelty, the beautiful story, or the ear-haunting melody is completed. Even then, this is polished and re-polished, at length resulting in a thing of beauty, if not a joy forever, that bears upon it the stamp of success.

The amateur author and composer too often fall short ot ccess through lack of patience and careful thought. The sire to finish and publish one's "effort" is overwhelmingly rong. Friends and admirers innocently deluge the proud eator with profuse words of too often exaggerated appreation and eulogy, actually convincing the unfortunate vicm (for such he is) that when the song is put through the inter's or publisher's hands, "nothing can stop it from inantly becoming the craze of the country." It appears in int, money is spent in seemingly wise channels, but popurity does not appear and the writers wonder why, often acing the blame on other shoulders when it should be alost entirely on their own.

Many a manuscript has been dropped into the waste paper isket of the publisher, or has had money expended on it by ie author, or composer, in getting same published, only to ie a miserable, and sometimes, instantaneous death. Yet iis composition may really have contained a good or original lea in either lyrics, melody, or, perhaps both. They had not een worked out by careful thought and attention to detail, owever, and this, as has already been stated, is a fatal overght in the making of a successful "popular" song.

A few hints as to some of the prevalent causes that lead ie inexperienced into the paths of disappointment and disster may conveniently be presented here.

Awkward "intervals"—that is, intervals that are either unnatural, and do not sing gracefully, but have a jarring ffect on the ear, and intervals that are far apart, should be irefully avoided in a melody, especially if they occur in uick succession, such as:

EXAMPLES.

(BAD)

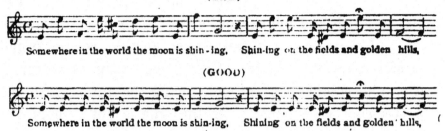

Somewhere in the world the moon is shin-ing. Shin-ing on the fields and golden hills,

(GOOD)

Somewhere in the world the moon is shin-ing, Shining on the fields and golden hills,

Also avoid using for singing a series of notes or tones which are so placed that the singer will be kept on the higher tones, such as the d's and c's and occasional f's. The untrained singer cannot produce a series of these tones without great strain, and finding this so, naturally takes little fancy to the song.

EXAMPLES.

(BAD)

She is the sweet-est girl I know, she's fair - est of them all,

(GOOD)

She is. the sweet - est girl I know, she's fair - est of them all,

If the reader will sing over these two examples in good and bad treatments of the use of high notes, he will find at once how much easier it is to sing the lower melody. The same range is used, but in the lower example it will be noted that after each high note the melody takes the voice downwards and immediately relieves the vocal strain. In the upper example, the singer is subjected to a sustained strain which grows in tension as the melody progresses.

Glaring imitation of known melodies should never be

countenanced by a composer who aims at success. To start with, it shows weakness in thought, and lack of self-reliance, individuality and originality.

Reminiscence in a slight degree in "popular" melodies is often a benefit, as it assists popularity in a new song. The untrained listener, for example, feels that he or she has "heard something that began like that before"; but it is so disguised that one cannot recall just precisely what it *is* like. Curiosity is thus aroused, the gentle critic keeps humming your melody in an effort to discover its original source, and the more it is hummed, or discussed, the closer it gets towards that much desired goal—Popularity.

Bare-faced imitation in melodies or styles, never, as a rule, succeeds. The public is a fickle quantity, ever looking for something new which it devours quickly when found. No sooner is its appetite appeased, than it grows tired of its former food and seeks something with a new flavor. "Iliawatha" was new in idea: the name, the atmosphere, the rhythm were all new, and instantly caught the public fancy. So tremendous a success was it that hundreds of writers, some good and many bad, lost no time in trying to secure financial benefit from this one new idea, and the musical market was flooded with Indian intermezzos of every kind and description. The rest died, literally unhonored and "unsung."

Many seemingly poorly written songs have achieved the greatest kind of popularity, but in every case, if the songs are analyzed by anyone versed in such matters, it will be found that either in lyrics, melody, or both, an original and novel idea that appealed to public fancy has existed. It is the knowledge of these little originalities that are needed, and where to place them properly, that the amateur song-writer should seek and try to become familiar with.

Whenever you find it difficult to continue satisfactorily in a melody you have commenced upon, or hard to remember a melody the second time you play, whistle, or sing it over, you can safely rely upon it that this is not the melody you want. Lay the work aside until some later time when you can formulate and work out some new idea that flows readily and easily, and that "sticks" to you right away. There will grow upon you then the pleasant conviction that this latter melody is the right one, and that no amount of further experimenting will ever make it otherwise.

Often, upon reading over a set of good lyrics, a melody will instantly formulate itself; you feel inspired, you sing it from beginning to end with almost the same ease as you would a familiar air; it almost talks the words. When a happy combination of circumstances like this, occurs it is safe to say that in ninety-nine cases out of a hundred it is an inspiration, and that it *is* the one and only melody for the lyric with which you wish to associate it.

Do not, however, think that your work is over when you have transferred this inspiration to paper. Far from it. It is here that the successful composer really starts. It is just as well to put your melody aside for a while; let your enthusiasm have time to grow cold; take it up again in a few days and see if it appeals to you as strongly as it did at first. See if it sings as easily, see if you have placed it in the right key for the best popular range —(this will be discussed in another chapter)—and see if your intervals are easily sung Discard any awkward accidentals, if possible,—remember the simpler it is the better the chance of real popularity. If you discover, after a strict analysis of all these ints, that your melody stands the test, and possesses all ese essentials, you may then rest absolutely assured that far you are on the right track.

Next comes the piano accompaniment to your melody. lis requires a careful amount of thought. It must be easy execution, it must lay under the fingers well, it must be ch in harmony, it must not, as a rule, contain chords of ore than three notes, or, at the most, four; it must not be ritten in difficult and unpopular keys, and it must be interting. Reference to the chapter that follows will explain e salient points which it is desirable to have in mind in riting an effective accompaniment.

CHAPTER III.

THE ACCOMPANIMENT.

Best keys to write in—Range of Melody—Different forms of Accompaniment.

The first thing to determine in writing accompaniments to a song is the key in which your melody is to be placed. There is, of course, no hard and fast rule as to what is and what is not a desirable key; for in this matter, as in all others, circumstances alter cases. The best key may be determined after due consideration as to whether the song is intended for, or most suitable to, a certain range or quality of voice which comprises the following well known divisions:

Soprano or Tenor (Range.)

Contralto or Baritone (Range.)

Basso (Range.)

It is not to be supposed, of course, that the music **for a** brilliant, sparkling waltz-song should be written to suit a voice of low range; or, again, that a swingy, stirring story of the sea, war, etc., should be set to a melody that suggests nothing but a high soprano voice, or any other equally similar unharmonious combination of lyrics and melody. Con-

quently the composer must exercise discretion in placing
is melody for the song in question in a range most adapted
o the proper rendition of the song and melody. The above
emarks are, perhaps, more important as applied to songs
oming under the heads of high class ballads, sacred songs,
nd those especially written for certain artists.

For the accepted various classes of popular songs, such
s Home, or Mother songs, Waltz, Coon, March songs, etc.,
here is practically a set limit of range, which is generally
etween "C" below the staff, and "E" on the staff. Thus:

Very rarely should a popular melody be set below or
bove these notes. The reason for this is, of course, that
opular songs are, for the most part, sung by the masses,
rho, as a whole, do not possess cultivated voices, and the
atural, untrained voice cannot produce tones outside of
he range given without great effort. Whatever is an effort
n the production or rendition of a popular song should be
liminated before its public appearance. Moreover, the
ange of notes given is ample for any effective melody. Some
f the tunes that have existed for centuries—the old "folk
ongs" of many lands—have all been encompassed within a
nuch more restricted range than the example quoted. In-
eed, many of the more popular songs of the day have melo-
ies that are comprised within six notes, say, "E" to "C,"
oth on the staff.

Popular songs written in the keys which have sharps
the sign for which is ♯) for their signature are not in
avor, excepting the key of G Major, which has one sharp, F,
or its signature. Experience has shown that for some

peculiar reason the masses, as well as quite a number of more or less educated musicians, do not finger or readily read music written in sharp keys. The following keys are the best to select from:

C Major (No Sharps or Flats).

G Major (One Sharp, F).

F Major (One Flat, B).

B Flat Major (Two Flats, B and E).

E Flat Major (Three Flats, B, E, and A).

For popular songs, where a soft or plaintive melody is desired, A Flat Major, (Four Flats, B. E. A and D) is useful.

Minor keys for melodies to pathetic, weird, mysterious or mock sentimental lyrics, can be used with beautiful and excellent effect. The usual Minor keys to be used in popular songs, are those which have the same signatures as the first five Major keys above mentioned, and are as follows:

A Minor (No Sharps or Flats).

E Minor (One Sharp, F).

D Minor (One Flat, B).

G Minor (Two Flats, B and E).

C Minor (Three Flats, B, E and A).

In each of the above keys, no matter which is used, the experienced composer of popular songs always keeps the melody within the accepted limited range, as already indicated. Occasionally, as in a big catchy march number, where a rousing climax is desired, an F or F Sharp above, is admissible, but if nothing is lost by avoiding such notes, so much the better.

Simplicity of accompaniment, with pretty harmonies, is a golden rule. Many an otherwise excellent popular song has been a failure because the accompaniment was too difficult for the majority to play easily. Remember, the patron of the popular song does not, as a rule, desire to exert any effort lu·its rendition. On the other hand, the reader must not suppose that a bald, uninteresting accompaniment should be the rule. The aim of the composer should be to retain the interest even in the accompaniment.

Arpeggios in a quick tempo, runs requiring skilful execution, quick jumps in either right or left hand, are to be avoided in accompaniments to popular songs. The ordinary pianist or accompanist discards the use of a song containing such features, because he lacks the necessary skill required for an adequate rendition.

A sudden change of key in a song is often very effective and brings a delightful surprise to the ear. This device will often relieve what would otherwise be a rather monotonous melody. Such sudden change, however, must be made to occur, as a rule, quite naturally and smoothly, and must

29

pass from the original key to its either relative Minor, or a change such as that illustrated, from "Love Laughs at Locksmiths," from the operatic success, "Sergeant Kitty:"

The signature of the key is not to be changed, **however, in** writing these deviations, but the accidentals (**Sharps or Flats**) must be used in front of the notes requiring same, in order to show exactly the change of key or the return into the original key. Where, however, the change of key **involves the** use of eight measures or more, it is better to change **the** signature, reverting to the original signature in its proper place. In this way, you simplify the process of reading the · song immensely.

Another rule which the popular song writer may usefully bear in mind is never to change the key of the chorus or refrain of a song; keep it in the same key as your verse is written in. This rule, indeed, is imperative, and even the composer whose desire is to be as original as he consistently can, must be careful that his zeal for new effects and his desire to depart from conventionality do not run away with his discretion in this respect.

A few suggestions regarding accompaniments for the main classes of popular songs may, perhaps, be useful and act as a guide to the amateur when considering the best form and style for certain songs.

HOME OR MOTHER SONGS.

DESCRIPTIVE, SENSATIONAL BALLADS.

Write these either in common, or 4-4 time, or 3-4 time; or else 4-4 time for the verse and 3-4 time for the refrain.

The Prelude, or Introduction, should usually comprise four measures of common time, or eight measures of 3-4 time, founded on, if not identical with, the opening bars of the verse melody and accompaniment, closing with a dominant chord, or occasionally a chord of the seventh. Another effective prelude can be constructed by similarly using the closing strain of the refrain. Except in songs of a strictly fanciful order, or dainty, high class compositions, where a prelude may often be independent, and only slightly suggestive of what follows, this rule should be adhered to. It serves the double purpose of introducing the theme of the song to its listeners and of acquainting the singer with the first few measures of the song, as occasionally he may forget the opening phrase.

A verse in common time is generally sixteen measures in length, and thirty-two measures if in 3-4 time. The refrain should be (a) common time, eight or sixteen measures; (b) ¾ time, sixteen or thirty-two measures.

Give the melody to the right hand, as this aids the voice materially, and use judgment in creating pretty effects by the addition of a second note, such as the third, or sixth, or octave. The left hand usually has a moving figure in arpeggio form combining the fundamental bass notes with the broken chords. Thus:

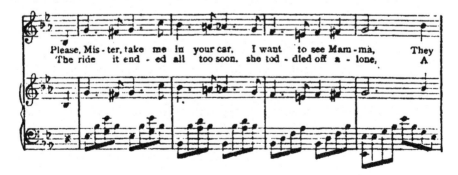

Please, Mis - ter, take me in your car, I want to see Mam - ma,
The ride it end - ed all too soon. she tod - dled off a - lone,
They
A

or it is written with the plain fundamental bass note, and following it are the one, two or three chords. More than three notes in the chords for the left hand are to be avoided:

Usually after the first eight measures of the verse the melody goes into the relative Minor key, or the key of the Dominant, and here the accompaniment is often varied, possibly by writing the right hand melody in octaves, or omitting the right hand melody entirely, both hands playing the simple chord harmony; or a counter melody is introduced in the right or left hand (although counter melodies in the popular songs are not usual). After the Minor four, or, most often, eight measures, the melody reverts to the original Major key and melody, closing either with the chord of the dominant, or, more often, one of the inversions of the chord of the seventh, so as to lead smoothly and naturally into the refrain.

"POPULAR" WALTZ SONGS.

Forms of accompaniments to this class of songs should usually be as follows:

The introduction should consist of eight measures, either taken from the first eight of the verse finishing on the dominant chord of the key, or the first four and last four of the

chọrus. The first four measures of the verse or chorus together with four concluding measures of easy and fanciful
melodic figure might also be employed if a spice of variety
will improve matters.

In the accompaniment of the verse the melody is given
to the right hand, with here and there an easy little run or
figure to fill out empty measures or to suggest orchestral
effects. For example:

This form continues in much the same style throughout
the chorus with perhaps the last eight measures of the right
hand (where the chorus is sixteen measures in length) or
the last sixteen measures (where the chorus is thirty-two

measures in length) of melody, written in octaves to give added force and brilliancy to the finish.

In "popular" waltz songs the chorus may be written with a first and second ending, as this style of refrain lends itself readily to repetition. The first ending should be written so that the accompaniment continues and leads back into the beginning of the chorus melody naturally and easily and without a break. Example:

In waltz movements, where the melody moves in dotted half notes, or a half note and a quarter note, such as the following example, an effective accompaniment is:

This form of accompaniment should not, however, be employed where the melody contains several notes in each measure, as the execution required for this is quite difficult and simplicity must always be the object in view.

It is usual when the harmony is carried in the left hand to write the fundamental bass notes of each measure in single notes and not as the octave. An exception to this may be made in the case of a passage marked "Forte," but here octaves should only be used either as half or quarter notes. Eighth or sixteenth notes in quick succession written in octave form for the left hand are too difficult of execution for use in "popular" waltz songs.

It must be borne in mind that in all waltz songs, and in fact in all other "popular" songs, the number of measures in the introduction or prelude, verse, and chorus or refrain, should invariably be either 4, 8, 16, 32, or 64. Introductions of over eight measures, verses over thirty-two, or refrains or choruses over thirty-two measures in Waltz, sixteen in Home, Mother and Descriptive Songs, are not desirable in the great majority of instances. In March, Coon or Production songs the refrain or chorus can be and usually is thirty-two measures in length, while the verses are either sixteen or not over thirty-two measures.

Coon Songs.

The introduction or prelude should comprise four, eight or sixteen measures finishing on the dominant or inversion of the seventh chord. Except where a "vamp" follows the eight measure introduction, the latter should run straight into the verse melody. A "vamp" may be composed of two measures (occasionally four) which are so formed that they can be played over and over again until the singer is ready to commence the verse. Two examples of a "vamp" are given: One from May Irwin's famous song "Albany,"

the other being taken from Ernest Hogan's great **shouting** song "Is Everybody Happy?"

These "vamps" are usually as varied as possible in melody and harmony, or are written to portray the style and atmosphere of the song. For instance, a Coon song which is mysterious or sad in story, and consequently similar in melody and accompaniment, should have a movement in the "vamp" suggestive also of same. A good example of this may be found in the "vamp" to the well known song "My Loving Henry."

The most simple form of "vamp" is often preferable, such as:

If no particular effect is desired but merely an appropriate "vamp," it will be found that quite often the first two measures of the verse melody may be very usefully employed. This form of "vamp" has the additional advantage of helping nervous singers to remember exactly how the song starts,—a very important point when you come to think of it.

Some Coon songs are better without "vamps" of any kind. This is a point that may well be left to the discretion of the composer.

To resume, the introduction is usually formed from the melody and accompaniment of either four or eight (if the song is in common time), or eight or sixteen measures (if in 2-4 time) of the beginning of the verse, or a combination of measures taken from the verse and refrain skilfully blended. If in common time, the verse should be sixteen measures in length with a refrain of equal length, having a first and second ending for repetition purposes.

If in 2-4 time the verse and refrain should consist of thirty-two measures each and the refrain should have a first and second ending as in the cases already referred to.

If either form of song has a "vamp," a *Dal Segno* (D. S.) sign, i. e.,

D.S. (˙$.)

is written at the end of the last measure of the refrain, which takes the accompaniment back to the beginning of the vamp, where a similar sign (˙$.) is placed. In such a case the original prelude or introduction is not, of course, played again. When the song has no "vamp" the accompaniment goes back to the beginning and the original prelude or introduction is played before singing the second or following verses.

It is usual to place at the finish of the chorus in these instances a *De Capo* mark, thus D. C. This leaves no room for doubt as to where the prelude and accompaniment for the second verse really start.

These are invariably written in either 2-4, Common (C or 4-4) time, or 6-8 time.

The introduction, if in 2-4 time, may be eight or sixteen measures in length ending with the dominant or seventh chord. It should lead into a simple "vamp" of two measures, marked "Till Ready." If in Common or 4-4 time, it should be four or eight measures, and finish in the same manner. If in 6-8 time, eight or occasionally sixteen measures may be written, the conclusion being either the dominant chord, leading directly into the verse melody, or into a simple, straight "vamp" of two measures, marked "Till Ready."

The theme of the introduction is generally founded on certain of the catchiest measures of the song, preferably the last strain of the chorus, as this acts as an effective variant as well as an appropriate interlude between the first chorus and the second verse.

The construction of the verse should be as follows :

If in 2-4 time 32 measures in length,
If in 4-4 time 16 measures in length.
If in 6-8 time 16 or 32 measures in length.

The refrain should consist of a corresponding number of measures, except in rare cases. First and second endings should be given here also for repeats, as well as the D.S., or D.C. signs, exactly as explained in a previous paragraph.

In the accompaniments to 2-4 movements, the melody is usually placed in the right hand, in an easy playable form so as to uphold the voice with plain octaves where force or brilliancy is desired in the refrain, as already mentioned.

A plain moving fundamental bass note, followed with the corresponding broken chord or chords is employed by the left hand, thus: (extracted from "Farewell, Sweetheart May.")

And till death I'll always love you, Farewell, sweetheart May........

In 4-4 March time, which is of course a slower tempo than 2-4, the accompaniment takes the form of giving the melody and harmony to the right hand, and fundamental bass octaves or single notes to the left hand. Thus:

Sweet - ly the mu - sic
Sounds of the big guns

play - ing, To the sound of the march-ing feet,..............
boom - ing, 'Mid the crash of the shot and shell,..............

In 6-8 or 2-4 movements, which are sprightly and joyous in character, the accompaniment can be written with either the plain melody in the right hand and the bass single note or octave with following chords in the left hand; or with the melody and harmony in the right hand and the fundamental bass single notes or octaves in the left hand. Both forms are here shown:

(A)

At the finish of each four or eight measure phrase in the accompaniment, there will be noticed a sort of pause that inevitably suggests the need of some "filling in" process. To accomplish this, one may employ with either the left or right hand, or both, some pretty figure, a little run, two or three chords, or something characteristic of the song. In a song of War, for instance, the introduction of certain bugle calls and the like are effective in this way. In a patriotic song a few notes of one of the National airs will please if neatly dovetailed into the accompaniment. All this, of course, must be left to the discretion and taste of the composer and arranger.

Comic or Topical Songs.

Accompaniments for topical songs depend entirely on the style, character and tempo of the melody. Whichever it is, reference to the forms and styles already described and shown in previous examples will be sufficient in practically all cases to form a satisfactory basis for the accompaniment and its most effective and appropriate treatment.

The chief thing is to remember that an accompaniment should be simple and bright, for in comic songs the words and melody are paramount and must be heard easily by the listener. The accompaniments therefore must not be such as to interrupt the pointed delivery of the words, or drown the melody.

Do not make the mistake that so many do of imagining that melody in a comic song is a secondary consideration. It is the lack of a good tune that ruins many a humorous song, just as indifferent words have ruined many an excel-

lent melody. It is quite possible to combine humor and mel.
lody; indeed, a little care and thought will often enable the
composer to absolutely echo in his music the laugh of the
line to which it is set. Little things like this sometimes make
all the difference between a hopeless failure and a big
money-making success.

The verse and refrain should be short. A long drawn
out verse and refrain is nearly always detrimental to the
success of a comic or topical song. Come to the point quick.
ly and let it be really amusing and comical. Finally, don't
write a comic song without a comic idea. This is a common
mistake that a lot of well-intentioned persons fall into, with
the result that their songs are comical without being comic.
This is a distinction not without a difference.

HIGH CLASS BALLADS AND SACRED SONGS.

The arrangement of the accompaniment for songs in this
class should not be attempted by the amateur. A considerable technical and theoretical knowledge is required for this
work if the ultimate result is to be of any artistic worth at
all.

The best plan is to get some thorough professional arranger to do this work in all cases. The amateur may be
capable enough in the composition of the melody by the
exercise of due care regarding range, phrasing, etc., but here
his ambition should cease until he has a practical knowledge
of harmony and composition at his fingers' ends. A thorough course in harmony, composition and thorough bass
should be undertaken before attempting accompaniments to
these styles of songs.

PRODUCTION SONGS.

Under this heading we will also include songs written for particular singers and artists. The term "production" song is used to denote a composition that is in all salient features most particularly adapted for use in a theatrical or musical production. It usually demands scenic surroundings, use of calcium or moonlight effects, etc., and is written with a view to the introduction of certain stage business or costume effects to be used by the singer or chorus behind the soloist. Or, again, it may involve the use of certain "properties" ("props") to insure its successful rendition. A publisher does not launch such songs on the public through the channel of ordinary advertisement or through the still more valuable advertising medium of the vaudeville stage or other public use. The demand for songs of this class is wholly created by their being placed in some metropolitan production, which if successful, tours the large cities of the country after the metropolitan run is concluded. Some well known artist renders the song and becomes in a large degree associated with it. The excellent "production" of the song, if meritorious, creates a quick demand for it on the part of the public, the melody is played in the cafes, hotels and restaurants, consequently becomes immensely popular, and finally is sung by everybody.

In writing "production" songs, both the writer of the lyrics and composer of the music must exercise considerable ingenuity and originality in devising a novelty, suggesting some pretty scene, calling for the introduction of striking and novel stage business. The words must be unusually catchy and the music haunting to the ear. It is beyond the scope of this brief treatise to enter into the numberless details and suggestions that could be given in reference to this class of song, both as regards suitable ideas, style, etc., in words, melody and accompaniment. There is no fixed rule whatever. In fact, a production "song" is really a small "production" in itself, and therefore should be, though unhappily it is often not so, a self-contained and independent creation, to which no particular rule or set of rules can be usefully applied. What suits one is inappropriate to another. Rules for production songs are dependent upon the "idea" of the song, and this little work lays no claim to be a universal provider of ideas which are the result in most cases of a happy inspiration or accident, whichever term seems the better under the circumstances.

Let the amateur watch the big hits of the metropolitan productions, and he will learn more than can ever be told in words regarding this fanciful and lucrative style of song-writing.

Waltz, Coon, March, Comic and Topical, Character or Dialect songs are, of course, quite frequently used in productions; but to be available for acceptance by managers or artists, they must be exceptionally well written both as regards words and melody, and must contain something more than that which is termed "ordinarily good."

CHAPTER IV.

FINISHING TOUCHES PREVIOUS TO PUBLICATION—SUBMITTING MSS. TO A PUBLISHER.

The song being completed in both lyrics and melody and accompaniment, the writer of the lyrics and the composer should confer together, play the song over on the piano, see that the words both in metre, feet (number of syllables) and accent throughout, fit the melody naturally and correctly, and vice versa. A well written song must fit both ways. If there are any questionable defects, study them over carefully and find a means to eradicate any such blemishes. Haste and impatience should never be allowed to influence the mind of the song writer who seeks success.

If possible, have your song "tried out" or sung at some public entertainment, concert, or amateur minstrel show. Here you can hear it sung by others than yourself, but do not let it be publicly known that you are the writer or writers of the song. You will then see how the song "goes" on its own merits. Some hitherto unseen or unsuspected defect may in this way possibly be discovered, and you are consequently able to correct it before the song goes to the printer or publisher. Remember that when your song is published and placed on sale it is too late to change it unless you do it very quickly and are willing to go to much extra expense. Be sure it is as good as you can possibly make it in all points before it leaves your hand.

Never let your song be printed or presented to an artist or a responsible publishing house unless the manuscript copy of the music be written in ink, in a good legible hand.

If you are not competent to do this, and few amateur or professional composers are, send it to some reliable person or firm that makes a business of writing and preparing manuscripts (*Mss.*) for professional use or publishing purposes.

A poorly written *Ms.* is always greatly handicapped. The artist or publisher cannot read or play it with ease, the accompaniment too often is not written in correct technical form, the words are not syllabled or placed rightly under the notes, and consequently interest is at once lost in an otherpossibly good piece of work.

Some folks appear to be under the impression that the average publisher sits all day in his chair wringing his hands in despair because he cannot find any songs to publish. These people therefore rush to his assistance and send him "music" to which nobody but a hard-hearted tomcat could possibly do justice. Don't emulate them. Send nothing but what has artistic merit, and let it be always properly presented and worth the trouble of examining. Depend on it a good looking *Ms.* will always receive conscientious attention, while not frequently an untidy or clumsy piece of work is never even given the chance of examination.

A prominent New York publishing house once received a *Ms.* by registered mail. It was a song, or at any rate, it purported to be. It was written on a large sheet of dirty yellow paper which had probably been used to take home Sunday's leg-of-mutton from the butcher's; the lines of the staff were all carefully drawn (it was the only careful thing about it) with a quarter inch space between each, and the notes were literally "shaded" in with a soft lead pencil, and looked like a heterogeneous collection of decayed duck's eggs. The composition was rejected. Another firm received a masterpiece written on a torn piece of brown paper the size of a bath towel. Of course the result to the respective composers was nil l

An extra typewritten set of the words should always accompany your complete M*ss.* when sent to artists, publisher or manager. Don't try to draw the design yourself for your title page when sending your *Ms.* to a publisher for his consideration, unless you are really an artist. If you wish some particular design that is original or specially desired, explain the subject clearly in words. It is always the best plan, however, to say nothing at all about it. The drawing of title pages is an art in itself, and the publisher knows better than any one else what design or style will bring the best results.

When writing an artist or a publisher requesting his consideration of your *Mss.,* one with a view to his using or singing it, the other in the hope that he may publish it and include it in his catalogue on royalty, have your letter typewritten if possible, and make it as brief and courteous as you can. The same remarks apply of course when submitting a *Ms.* to a manager for use in his production. These people are always very busy, so don't do anything to waste their time. Enclose addressed and stamped envelope for reply.

Never send your original *Ms.* copy to any one. Have several copies made, so that if for any reason a *Ms.* is lost or not returned promptly, you are able to continue your promotion of the song by the use of your other copies

CHAPTER V.

Printing and Publishing Your Own Composition.

Many authors and composers prefer to publish and promote their own compositions rather than place them with a publisher on "royalty" (a percentage on the sale).

The main reason for so doing is undoubtedly that the owner may secure the entire revenue and profits resulting from publication and sale. There are numberless firms who make a business of printing, or who can contract for same, and it is well to warn those who desire to be their own publishers that they should investigate the reputation, style of work, and promptness of the firm with whom they place their orders, unless of course the firm is of solid standing and prestige which insures satisfaction and is a fact that may be readily ascertained.

Several firms seem to presume that the amateur publisher, being ignorant of fair and current prices for copyrighting, arranging and printing music, etc., or of the necessary quality of such work for successful use, presents what might almost be termed "an easy mark." Such firms offer very low prices and estimates and the amateur is often lured into placing his work and order with one of them, the result of course bringing great dissatisfaction and often regrettable disaster.

The importance therefore of exercising care and judgment in the selection of your prospective printing house is apparent. Ascertain from reliable source its standing, reputation and the quality of work with which it is identified, before placing your orders.

Remember that first class work demands just and reasonable prices, and a few extra dollars put into the work will more than repay the outlay in results, general satisfaction and success.

Let us assume that the prospective firm has been decided on. A letter should be written requesting an estimate on your Ms. (a copy of which should be enclosed) for printing a certain number of copies. If the firm also makes a specialty (which, however, very few such firms do) of editing, and copyrighting, etc., and these necessary points regarding your *Ms.* have not already been attended to, you should further request that in the estimate these details be added and figured in.

It is far better to have one firm take the entire matter in hand, as the result will always be more satisfactory, provided, of course, you select a firm which makes a specialty of covering this class of work from start to finish.

The estimate being duly received, considered and found satisfactory, write your acceptance, at the same time requesting that your order shall be delivered to you at a certain date. Thirty days is usually sufficient for a reliable firm to complete the order.

When the copies are received (the plates by the way being usually retained by the printer, who keeps them in a fireproof vault for your safety, and thus facilitates matters when you desire a second edition printed) the amateur publisher naturally seeks to discover the best means to attract public attention and promote popularity for the composition.

Some suggestions for assisting towards a solution of this interesting problem will doubtless be of value.

In the first place, the local music dealers or department

stores must be considered. Take a sample copy, see the buyers; if possible play the composition over for them, offer the first order for copies at what is termed an "Introductory" rate, which is usually 10c. per copy, and request them to display and push the music to the best advantage. Future orders for your composition should be sold to the trade for from 12½ to 15 cents a copy, presuming of course that the marked price on the cover of your composition is 50 cents (usually designated by a figure 5). This marked price is customary on all popular songs.

Secondly, there are the music teachers, who provide an excellent medium for disposing of your composition, assuming, of course, that it is of a character suitable for or adapted to the requirements of pupils or their public use of same.

Thirdly, advertise in the papers and trade magazines. This medium is generally a very useful one. A neat and happily worded article inserted in your daily paper or papers describing the composition, the author and composer, the artist or artists who are singing the song, or those who will use it at a coming public entertainment, will attract great attention; and if the composition is a song, a cut showing all or a portion of the chorus or refrain, both words and melody, will greatly increase the chances of creating a good local demand.

An attractive advertisement placed in one or more of the recognized musical trade papers, such as

> The Music Trades
> The Music Trade Review
> Musical America
> The Musical Age

all of which organs devote several pages of each issue to sheet music and music publishers, will gain the attention of

the sheet music dealers throughout the country in a gene
way. All these periodicals are published in New York.

Local promotion, however, and your own personal effo
earnestly exerted in the direction of making the compositi
the "popular" hit of your particular city or locality, are
best means after all, for if the piece has merit and you c
trive to have it sung and played at every conceivable oppe
tunity, it will spread rapidly, news of it will be carried
other towns and cities, some one will sing it there, oth
will want copies, and a sort of endless chain is set in moti

As soon as your composition shows signs of recogniti
by the public, and conseqüently of possessing the essenti
of popularity, it is a good plan to expend a little more mo
in having it arranged for orchestra or brass band, or bo
and then printed in this form.

If your composition is a song, have it arranged in so
popular dance form such as a waltz, two-step or schottisc
for orchestra. A skilful arranger who is accustomed to su
work can readily adapt any style of popular song to one
other of the above mentioned forms of dancing. This bei
done, secure a list of the names and addresses of all the lo
band and orchestra leaders. Mail to each of them a cop
accompanied by a neat and concise note requesting them
play the piece at all their dances and engagements.
programs are used, ask them to print the title on san
Should your composition show signs of popularity arou
town, these leaders will be only too glad to play the ;
rangement.

But remember a *good* arrangement for either brass ba
or orchestra is imperative. Some arrangers are adepts
preparing a composition for large orchestras, but the ;

rangement is absolutely useless for the small ones. The argument applies equally well the other way. These arrangements to be effective and to do the composition justice, must be written to suit both the large and very small organizations, and only a skilful professional arranger accustomed to this work should be consulted.

CHAPTER VI.

Presenting *Mss.* to a Publishing House for Publication.
Selling Outright. Royalties.

If the author and composer feel that they are not prepared to publish and handle their composition personally and to achieve success, there is always the other medium— the regular publisher of music.

Compositions to be presented to a publisher should be expertly arranged or edited, and neatly written in proper form. A brief letter should accompany your *Mss.*, couched in terms similar to the following:

Messrs. Jones & Smith,

New York City.

Dear Sirs: Enclosed herewith please find M*s.* of my composition entitled "................," which I desire to place with your firm on royalty. Kindly give same your attention and consideration, and if available for your catalogue, advise me and send contracts for my signature. If unavailable, return *Ms.* for which I enclose necessary postage.

Very truly yours,

John Blank.

If you desire to sell your composition outright, word your letter as follows:

Messrs. Jones & Smith,

New York City.

Dear Sirs: Enclosed herewith please find *Ms.* of my composition entitled "................", which I desire to sell outright. Kindly give same your consideration, and if agreeable to you, state your best cash offer. If unavailable for your catalogue, return *Ms.* at your early convenience for which I enclose necessary postage. Awaiting your favors, I remain,

Very truly yours,

John Blank.

If you wish to stipulate a certain price at the outset, mention it. Furthermore, should you have already printed and published your piece, and should it have attained a certain measure of popularity, and you desire to sell outright, mention to what extent the composition has caught on, and give reference of your local music dealers, etc.

The usual course to pursue in the case of an unpublished *Ms.* is to place it with a publisher on a royalty basis. If the song is successful, this arrangement always results much more satisfactorily to the author from a financial standpoint.

"Royalty," it should be explained, is a certain stipulated percentage given the owner or owners of a *Ms.* on all sales of the composition during the life of the copyright. Copies issued by the publisher as "new issues," that is to say, copies sent to the trade at a very low price as a means of introducing same, also enabling the music dealer, shou he have a call for the piece, to have one or more copies hand so that he may know that the piece is published a by whom; also the copies that are given away to professi al singers, soiled copies, etc., are not, of course, includ among those on which royalty is paid. It is needless to a that a reliable publisher invariably exercises a judicio control as regards the circulation and disposition of cop on which there is no royalty given.

By placing your composition with a publisher of mu you are relieved of all expense and speculation and the ti that would otherwise be devoted to its promotion and s is saved. The publisher, after acceptance of your compo tion, assumes entire control of it and everything connect with it, from the time of its acceptance to the day on whi it appears on the market. Having at his command countl channels and avenues for its exploitation and sale, he stan in a far better position to promote success for a good co position than the private individual could ever hope attain.

Royalty contracts offered by the representative publis ers differ in many of their minor points, but their gener and main features are nearly all the same.

Two cardinal points to be looked into when a contract offered and received for your signature are:

(a) The amount of royalty offered; and,

(b) A time limit for the publication of "regular" copi (that is the copies offered for sale) to be set, that if the composition is not published with the period stipulated (usually six months) t owner of the Ms. is at liberty to dispose of it els where and the Ms. will be returned to him on d mand.

The sum of 5 cents (or 10 per cent.) was, and in some cases still is, the usual amount of royalty offered in contracts upon each copy sold at regular rates as above described. During the past few years this was equitable enough, and the publisher of "popular" music was able to pay it. Recently, however, competition has become so keen that wholesale prices have dropped. The expenses in connection with the placing of compositions before the public and their general promotion, in many cases involving nothing short of absolutely forcing their popularity, now constitute so much heavier an item of cost that no honest publisher can afford to pay five cents a copy on compositions taken on royalty.

It is far more satisfactory, therefore, and adds much to the peace of mind of both author and composer to accept a royalty of 3 cents per copy, or even less.

Statements of royalty are usually rendered every three or six months. These periods are not calculated from the date of the publication of the composition, but are computed from January the 1st of each year, thus,—the 1st of April, July, October and January, on quarterly statements; and the 1st of July and January on half-yearly statements.

In placing compositions on royalty with publishers a transfer of or sole right to the copyright of the composition is invariably demanded by the publisher. Occasionally the composition is bought outright by the publisher. Where this arrangement obtains, the author and composer are required to sign a bill of sale or an assignment paper. In this they release all their right, title and interest in the said composition to the publisher or purchaser. A composition offered in this way to a publisher does not command any great amount of money, for the reason that all untried M*ss.*

are an unknown quantity and no one can positively predict either their future success or failure. Should the owner or owners of the composition in question have succeeded in placing it with some well known artist or performer, or with some first-class metropolitan production, and proof is furnished the publisher that the composition will be positively sung and produced in this manner, the value of the piece is at once somewhat enhanced. But it is just as well to remember that the good old adage, ''What is sauce for the goose is sauce for the gander,'' admirably adapts itself in the case of author or composer and publisher.

A reliable publisher will not accept your *Mss.* if he does not think that there is a reasonable possible chance of success for them. Success for the publisher means success financially for you. Incidentally, your reputation as a writer is brought to the front, which naturally counts for a good deal to you. Reputation, however, will avail nothing if the quality of your work does not at all times back it up. It is far better to write two or three songs that are really good and novel in all points than to ''manufacture'' an endless stream of *Mss.* of merely mediocre quality.

CHAPTER VII.

Hints and Don'ts.

Watch your competitors. Note their success or failure; analyze the cause and profit thereby.

Note public demand.

If you do not feel confident to write or compose a certain style of song, stick to the kind you are sure of, and gradually, adapt yourself to the others, if possible, before publicly presenting your work.

Avoid slang and vulgarism; they never succeed.

Avoid many-syllabled words ~~and those~~ containing hard consonants, wherever possible.

In writing lyrics be concise; get to your point quickly and when you arrive there make the point as strong as possible.

Simplicity in melody is one of the great secrets of success.

Let your melody musically convey the character and sentiment of the lyrics.

Don't try and write your music with a fine pointed pen. Use either a stub or a three-pointed music pen.

Don't use blotting paper on your written composition; let the ink dry.

Use a good black ink for writing. You can buy regular Music Ink at any good stationer's.

Try and acquire a good hand for writing music. If you find you cannot accomplish this or acquire the knack with any degree of satisfaction, let some one do this who is competent.

A poorly written manuscript is always handicapped when presented to a publisher, artist or manager.

Use good music paper. Cheap paper is never satisf
tory; the ink dries through and shows on the reverse si
If it be necessary to scratch or erase any of your writin
is practically impossible to write on the erased portion
a cheap paper again without hopelessly blurring the wh
thing.

In syllabling your words under the notes, the divisi
are not always made according to Webster, but are ve
often ruled by the way the respective divisions sound wl
sung. The following examples of five words selected at r
dom will show the difference in syllabling words in son

| *Webster* ——— | Mus - ic | · Stor - y | Re - cord | Sail · |
| *Vocal division* — | Mu - sic | Sto - ry | Rec - ord | Sai - |

Prom - en - ade
Prom - e - nade

Some composers in writing their manuscripts use rep
marks for measures which are exactly similar in either
treble or bass clef to the preceding measure or measu
Thus:

or, where two measures in both treble and bass clefs are
actly similar to the two preceding measures, the follow
form of repeat mark is used :

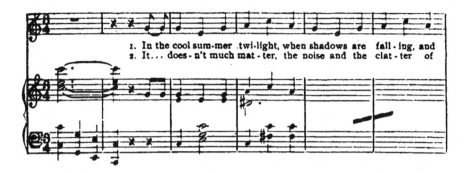

1. In the cool sum-mer twi-light, when shadows are fall-ing, and
2. It... does-n't much mat-ter, the noise and the clat-ter of

It is, however, always better to avoid the use of these devices. Write everything out just as it should appear in printed form. No mistakes can then arise.

When writing "popular" songs, always remember that it is the masses, the untrained musical public, to whom you must largely look for support and popularity. Don't, therefore, offer them anything which in subject or melody does not appeal to their ear. It is so much time thrown away if you do.

When you write to or visit a publisher, don't worry him with a history of what you have written or accomplished. He cares nothing about it, for no matter how many successes you may have had, or how popular your name may have become, if the composition which you offer does not possess the merits he regards as necessary, your former successes will not make your present offering of any greater value than that which would attach to the work of an utterly unknown writer.

If a publisher tells you coldly that he cannot use your composition, do not show or feel that you are hurt; and do not make the foolish mistake of telling him that he evidently does not know a good composition when he sees one. Even if he may suffer from so great a misfortune, recollect that

he is the purchaser and the party who has to invest th
money. It is therefore his privilege to accept or refuse
and it is his judgment that counts and nobody else's. A
ways be gracious and polite, for you never know how soo
you may need one's interest and good will in some othe
connection.

Don't be in a hurry.

Don't think that everything you write is a "sure hit."
Neither you nor anyone else knows the outcome until th
public pronounces the verdict.

Don't let your vanity get the upperhand of you. Ofte
an outside suggestion properly considered will be of ines
timable value.

Don't be "penny wise and pound foolish." If with th
outlay of a few more dollars you can enhance the value o
your work out of all proportion to the extra money investec
it will surely be a case, if ever there was one, of money we
spent.

Don't forget to enclose a separate typewritten set of th
words, if your Ms. be a song.

Don't get too easily discouraged. If at first you don
succeed, try again.

Don't give up "pushing" your song until it has ha
every chance. Remember that because you or your in
mediate friends have grown tired of it through familiarit
there are thousands and thousands to whom it is still
novelty.

Don't, when your name at last appears on the title pag
of a piece of music, sit all day admiring it. Get out an
hustle. Let others do the admiring. It is much more e
fective.

Finally, don't fold your Mss. when mailing them. Eithe
roll them or place them flat between paste-boards.

How to Copyright.

If you desire to copyright your own composition or any other piece of music, address a letter to the Librarian of Congress, Copyright Office, Washington, D. C., and kindly request him to mail you one or more Application Copyright Registration Blanks, which he will send you free of charge. Directions for filling out Application Blanks and fullest information on how to proceed to obtain correct coyprights for your compositions will be found upon the back of the Blank. Entry fee for a composition is 50c.; Certificate fee 50c. extra; making a total of One Dollar.

The law explicitly requires, in addition, the transmission of a printed copy of the title, which must be sent with the Application in order to insure entry of copyright. If typewritten title is sent it will be used, but at the risk of the applicant. No entry can be made upon a written title. Preferably the printed title cover of music should be sent, when this contains complete title with names of author of the words and composer or arranger of the music and the instrumentation. Typewritten titles are accepted upon the sole responsibility of the sender.

The law also requires, in addition to the entry of title, the deposit of two complete copies of the best edition of the work itself, not later than the day of publication in this or any foreign country.

Copies of the blank application forms can be obtained as stated above. Make requests for blank forms in separate communications, not as part of a letter relating to other copyright business.

Remittances should always be made preferably by money order, or by express order or blank draft. Currency or coin should not be sent, and checks only upon special arrangement with the Register of Copyrights. Postage stamps should under no circumstances be sent for copyright fees.

DICTIONARY OF RHYMES

DICTIONARY OF RHYMES

A, compare ER, OR

AB

cab	tab
crab	drab
dab	gab
nab	grab
slab	scab
stab	

AC, ACK

back	cardiac
black	maniac
clack	zodiac
claque	demoniac
crack	elegiac
hack	sac
knack	sack
lac	slack
lack	smack
pack	stack
plaque	tack
quack	track
attack	whack
lilac	wrack
nick-nack	arrack
almanac	

ACE

ace	lace
base	mace
brace	pace
case	place

ACE—Cont.

plaice	misplace
race	ecklace
space	outlace
trace	outpace
abase	replace
apace	retrace
birthplace	solace
debase	surface
deface	terrace
disgrace	unlace
embrace	interlace
chase	populace
dace	displace
face	efface
grace	grimace
horserace	

ACH, ATCH

batch	smatch
catch	snatch
hatch	swatch
latch	thatch
match	attach
patch	despatch
ratch	detach
scratch	

ACHE (see AKE)

ACT

act	fract
fact	pact

ACT—Cont.

tact	infract
tract	protract
attract	react
co-act	refract
compact	retract
contact	diffract
contract	subact
detract	subtract
abstract	transact
distract	cataract
enact	counteract
epact	incompact
exact	precontract
extract	re-enact
impact	

Also the preterites of verbs
in **ack**, as tack'd.

AD

add	pad
bad	plaid
brad	rad
clad	sad
fad	shad
gad	wad
glad	dryad
had	footpad
lad	monad
mad	salad

ADE

aid	made
bade	maid
blade	raid
braid	shade
cade	spade
fade	trade
glade	persuade
grade	pervade
jade	relaid
lade	tirade

AFT

aft	raft
craft	shaft
draft	waft
draught	abaft
graft	ingraft
haft	handicraft

Also the preterites of verbs in **aff, augh,** as quaff'd.

AG

bag	quag
brag	rag
cag	sag
crag	scrag
drag	shag
fag	slag
flag	stag
gag	swag
hag	tag
jag	wag
knag	tag-rag
lag	zig-zag
nag	

AGE, compare IDGE

age	passage
cage	peerage
gage	potage
gauge	presage
page	salvage
rage	sausage
sage	scutage
stage	village
swage	wreckage
wage	appanage
adage	appendage
assuage	disengage
baggage	equipage
mirage	cabbage
mortgage	corsage

AGE, compare IDGE—Cont.

cortege	heritage
courage	hermitage
cribbage	parentage
dotage	parsonage
engage	pasturage
enrage	patronage
hostage	percentage
marriage	personage
manage	pilgrimage
menage	villanage
message	concubinage
foliage	

AID (see ADE)

AIL—ALE

ale	detail
bail	entail
bale	exhale
brail	female
dale	pail
fail	pale
flail	quail
frail	rail
gale	sail
grail	sale
hail	scale
hale	shale
jail	snail
mail	stale
male	swale
nail	tail
wail	tale
wale	trail
whale	vale
assail	veil
avail	impale
blackmail	prevail
bewail	regale
curtail	retail

wholesale farthingale
aventail nightingale
countervail

AIM—AME

aim tame
blame acclaim
came became
claim declaim
dame defame
fame disclaim
flame exclaim
frame inflame
game misname
lame nickname
maim proclaim
name reclaim
frame surname
same overcame
shame

AIN—ANE

bane pane
blain plain
brain plane
cane rain
chain reign
crane rein
deign sane
drain skein
fain slain
fane sprain
feign stain
gain strain
grain swain
lain thane
lane train
main twain
mane vain
pain vane

vein explain
wain henbane
wane maintain
abstain murrain
amain obtain
arraign ordain
attain pertain
campaign profane
champagne refrain
complain regain
constrain remain
contain restrain
curtain retain
detain sustain
disdain appertain
distrain entertain
domain hurricane
enchain

AINT

faint complaint
feint mayn't
quaint plaint
saint constraint
taint distraint
acquaint restraint
attaint

AIR—ARE

air flare
bare gare
bear glair
care glare
chair hair
dare hare
e'er heir
ere lair
fair mare
fare ne'er

70

AIR—ARE—Cont.

pair	aware
pare	beware
pear	coheir
scare	compare
share	declare
snare	despair
spare	elsewhere
square	ensnare
stair	forbear
stare	forswear
swear	howe'er
tare	impair
tear (verb)	prepare
there	repair
ware	whate'er
wear	whene'er
where	where'er
yare	debonnair
affair	howsoe'er
armchair	millionaire

AIRS—ARES

theirs   unawares

And the plurals of nouns and the third persons singular of verbs in are, air, eir; as mares, repairs.

AISE—AZE

blaze	phrase
craze	praise
daze	raise
feaze	raze
gaze	amaze
glaze	cross-ways
graze	paraphrase
maze	

Also the plurals of nouns, and the third person singular of verbs in ay, ey, eigh; as lays, obeys, weighs.

AIT—ATE

bait	calculate
bate	candidate
date	captivate
eight	castigate
fate	celebrate
gait	celibate
gate	circulate
grate	congregate
great	consecrate
hate	contemplate
late	cultivate
mate	dedicate
pate	delegate
plate	delicate
prate	deprecate
rate	slate
sate	straight
irate	strait
migrate	wait
narrate	abate
prostrate	await
rebate	belate
relate	collate
sedate	create
translate	cremate
abdicate	debate
abrogate	dilate
accurate	elate
adequate	estate
advocate	frustrate
aggravate	ingrate
agitate	innate
alienate	desolate
animate	desperate
anotate	dislocate
antedate	dissipate
apostate	educate
arbitrate	elevate
arrogate	emigrate
aspirate	emulate
cachinate	estimate

extricate
formulate
fornicate
fortunate
generate
hesitate
hibernate
imitate
immolate
impetrate
imprecate
innovate
instigate
intimate
intricate
irritate
inundate
magistrate
meditate
micturate
mitigate
moderate
nominate
obstinate
oscillate
passionate
penetrate ⌄
perforate
perpetrate
personate
derogate
predicate
profligate
propagate
regulate
reprobate
ruminate
rusticate
separate
stipulate
subjugate

suffocate
syndicate
terminate
tete-a-tete
titivate
tolerate
triturate
vindicate
violate
abominate
accelerate
eccentuate
accommodate
accumulate
adulterate
affectionate
annihilate
anticipate
articulate
assassinate
capacitate
capitulate
chalybeate
coagulate
commemorate
commiserate
communicate
compassionate
inveterate
inviolate
legitimate
matriculate
necessitate
participate
precipitate
predestinate
predominate ⌄
premeditate
prevaricate
procrastinate
potentate

confederate
congratulate
considerate
contaminate
co-operate
corroborate
debilitate
degenerate
deliberate
⌇ denominate
depopulate
disconsolate
⌄ discriminate
effeminate
elaborate
emancipate
emasculate
equivocate
eradicate
evaporate
exaggerate
exasperate
expectorate

expostulate
exterminate
facilitate
illiterate
illuminate
immoderate
importunate
inanimate
initiate
insatiate
intemperate
intimidate
intoxicate
invalidate
investigate
prognosticate
recriminate
regenerate
reiterate
reverberate
subordinate
unfortunate

AITH, ATH (see EATH)

AKE, compare EAK

ache
bake
brake
break
cake
drake
fake
flake
hake
lake
make
quake
rake

sake
shake
snake
spake
stake
steak
take
wake
awake
bespake
betake
corn-crake
forsake

keepsake	partake
mandrake	overtake
mistake	snowflake
namesake	undertake

AL

pal	capital
shall	cardinal
cabal	carnival
canal	comical
cymbal	conjugal
dismal	cordial
dual	corporal
equal	criminal
feudal	critical
final	decimal
formal	festival
legal	funeral
loyal	general
martial	genial
medal	hospital
metal	inimical
mettle	initial
mortal	interval
naval	liberal
partial	literal
pedal	littoral
portal	madrigal
rival	magical
regal	medical
royal	mineral
rural	municipal
total	musical
trivial	mystical
admiral	natural
animal	nocturnal
annual	octagonal
arsenal	pastoral
autumnal	pedestal
cannibal	personal

physical	hymeneal
principal	imperial
prodigal	intellectual
rational	original
seneschal	poetical
several	political
sepulchral	problematical
temporal	prophetical
terminal	reciprocal
tragical	rhetorical
whimsical	satirical
colloquial	sempiternal
dogmatical	schismatical
equinoctial	tyrannical
equivocal	

ALD

bald	piebald
scald	emerald

Also the preterites of verbs
in **all, awl;** as call'd, bawl'd.

ALE (see AIL)

ALF (see AFF)

ALK—AUK, compare ORK

auk	mawk
balk	stalk
baulk	talk
calk	walk
chalk	tomahawk
hawk	

ALL

awl	call
ball	caul
bawl	crawl
brawl	drawl

ALL—Cont.

fall	stall
gall	tall
hall	thrall
haul	trawl
mall	wall
pall	appal
scrawl	enthral
shawl	football
small	install
sprawl	waterfall
squall	windfall

ALM (see ARM)

ALT

fault	asphalt
halt	assault
malt	default
salt	exalt
vault	

ALVE

calve	salve
halve	

AM

cram	beldam
dam	madam
cam	quondam
clam	wigwam
damn	malgam
dram	diagram
ham	diaphragm
jamb	epigram
lamb	monogram
ram	oriflamb
sham	telegram
swam	parallelogram
bedlam	

AME (see AIM)

AMP

camp	scamp
champ	stamp
clamp	swamp
cramp	vamp
damp	decamp
lamp	encamp

AN

ban	artisan
bran	barracan
can	caravan
clan	charlatan
fan	christian
man	courtesan
pan	musician
plan	ottoman
ran	partisan
scan	pelican
span	publican
swan	cosmopolitan
tan	attitudinarian
van	latitudinarian
wan	organ
began	orphan
divan	pagan
foreran	sedan
trepan	platitudinarian
unman	

ANCE

chance	balance
dance	enhance
glance	consonance
lance	countenance
prance	defiance
trance	dissonance
advance	ignorance
askance	importance

ANCE—Cont.

maintenance	circumstance
ordinance	complaisance
purveyance	concordance
sufferance	temperance
sustenance	utterance
expanse	vigilance
intrance	deliverance
mischance	exorbitance
romance	extravagance
seance	exuberance
ambulance	inheritance
arrogance	intemperance

ANCH

blanch	paunch
branch	ranche
ganch	stanch
haunch	carte-blanche
launch	

AND

band	command
bland	demand
brand	disband
gland	exband
grand	withstand
hand	contraband
land	countermand
sand	deodand
stand	reprimand
strand	understand
wand	

ANE (see AIN)

ANG

bang	gang
clang	hang
fang	pang

ANG—Cont.

slang	harangue
swang	rang
twang	sang

ANGE

change	arrange
grange	estrange
range	exchange
strange	interchange

ANK

bank	rank
blank	shank
crank	slank
drank	spank
frank	stank
hank	thank
plank	disrank
prank	mountebank
clank	

ANSE (see ANCE)

ANT

ant	adamant
aunt	arrogant
cant	combatant
chant	complaisant
grant	consonant
pant	conversant
plant	cormorant
rant	covenant
slant	disputant
remnant	dissonant
servant	dominant
supplant	elegant
tenant	elephant
transplant	ignorant

ANT—Cont.

jubilant	poignant
lieutenant	protestant
militant	recreant
:aslant	recusant
displant	ruminant
enchant	termagant
gallant	vigilant
implant	visitant
merchant	exorbitant
mordant	extravagant
rampant	inhabitant
recant	predominant
miscreant	significant
petulant	

AP

cap	pap
chap	rap
clap	sap
dap	scrap
flap	slap
gap	snap
hap	strap
lap	tap
map	trap
nap	wrap
enwrap	entrap
mishap	

APE

ape	nape
cape	rape
chape	scape
crape	scrape
drape	shape
grape	tape
jape	escape

APH (see AFF)

APSE

lapse	perhaps
elapse	relapse

Also the plurals of nouns, and the third person singular of verbs in ap; as maps, raps.

APT

apt	adapt

Also the preterites of verbs in ap; as rapp'd.

AQUE (see ACK)

AR

are	felspar
bar	friar
car	guitar
char	hookah
far	hussar
jar	liar
mar	mortar
pa	nectar
par	unbar
scar	angular
spar	avatar
star	calendar
tar	caviare
war	cinnabar
afar	popular
bazaar	regular
briar	secular
cellar	scimitar
catarrh	singular
cigar	titular
collar	vinegar
debar	particular
durbar	perpendicular

ARB

barb   rhubarb
garb

ARCE—ARSE

farce   sparse
parse

ARCH, compare ARK and

ARSH

arch   parch
larch   starch
march   countermarch

ARD

bard   custard
card   dastard
guard   discard
hard   dotard
lard   drunkard
nard   leopard
shard   niggard
sward   petard
ward   regard
yard   renard
bastard   retard
blackguard   vineyard
blizzard   wizard
bombard   disregard
charade   interlard
coward

Also the preterites of verbs
in ar; as barr'd.

ARF (see AFF)

ARGE

barge   large
charge   marge

ARGE—Cont.

discharge   o'ercharge
enlarge   surcharge

ARK

arc   shark
ark   spark
bark   stark
cark   embark
clerk   monarch
dark   remark
lark   hierarch.
mark   heresiarch
park

ARL

carl   parle
gnarl   snarl
marl

ARM

arm   becalm
balm   calm
barm   charm
harm   farm
palm   disarm
psalm   gendarme
qualm   salaam
alarm

ARN

barn   tarn
darn   yarn

ARP

carp   sharp
harp   counterscarp

ARSH (see also ARCH)

harsh   marsh

ART

art	start
cart	tart
dart	apart
hart	braggart
heart	depart
mart	dispart
part	impart
smart	counterpart

ARTH (see EARTH)

ARVE

carve   starve

AS

ass	amass
brass	cuirass
class	harass
crass	morass
grass	repass
lass	surpass
mass	coup de grace
pass	embarrass
alas	erysipelas

ASE (see ACE)

ASH

ash	dash
bash	flash
brash	gash
cash	gnash
clash	hash
crash	lash

ASH—Cont.

mash	slash
pash	smash
plash	thrash
rash	trash
sash	abash

ADK

ask	flask
bask	hask
cask	mask

ASM

chasm	sarcasm
spasm	cataplasm
miasm	enthusiasm
phantasm	protoplasm

ASP

asp	grasp
clasp	hasp
gasp	rasp

ASS (see AS)

AST

blast	avast
cast	bombast
caste	forecast
fast	repast
mast	outcast
last	overcast
past	enthusiast
vast	iconoclast
aghast	

Also the preterites of verbs in ass: as mass'd.

ASTE

baste	waste
chaste	distaste
taste	haste
waist	paste

Also the preterites of verbs in ace, ase; as lac'd, chas'd.

AT

bat	sat
brat	spat
cat·	sprat
chat	tat
fat	that
flat	vat
gnat	cravat
hat	cushat
mat	polecat
pat	acrobat
rat	

ATCH (see ACH)

ATE (see AIT)

ATH (see EATH)

ATHE (see EATHE)

AUB (see OB)

AUD

bawd	abroad
broad	applaud
fraud	defraud
laud	

Also the preterites of verbs in aw; as caw'd.

AUGH (see AFF)

AUGHT (see AFT—ORT)

AUK (see ALK)

AUN (see AWN)

AUNT, compare ANT

daunt	taunt
flaunt	haunt
gaunt	vaunt
jaunt	avaunt

AUSE—AUZE

cause	pause
clause	applause
gauze	because

Also the plurals of nouns, and the third person singular of verbs in aw; as laws, caws.

AVE

brave	shave
cave	slave
clave	stave
crave	wave
gave	behave
grave	deprave
knave	engrave
lave	forgave
nave	margrave
pave	outbrave
rave	architrave
save	

AW

chaw	flaw
claw	gnaw
craw	haw .
daw	jaw
draw	law

maw	cat's-paw
paw	guffaw
raw	hawhaw
saw	jackdaw
squaw	withdraw
straw	overawe
thaw	usquebaugh
foresaw	

AWL (see ALL)

AWN compare ORN

awn	pawn
brawn	prawn
dawn	spawn
drawn	yawn
fawn	withdrawn
lawn	

AX

axe	gimcracks
flax	poll-tax
lax	nicknacks
tax	relax
wax	thorax
borax	parallax
climax	

Also the plurals of nouns, and the third person singular of verbs in **ak**; as backs, lacks.

AY

aye	eh?
bray	fay
clay	flay
day	fray
dray	gay

grey	bewray
hay	convey
jay	decay
lay	defray
may	delay
neigh	denay
pay	dismay
play	display
pray	essay
prey	gainsay
ray	horseplay
say	hurrah
slay	inveigh
spray	levee
stay	obey
stray	portray
sway	purvey
they	relay
tray	repay
tway	soiree
way	subway
weigh	survey
whey	tramway
affray	dejeuner
allay	disarray
array	disobey
astray	matinee
away	roundelay
ballet	stowaway
belay	runaway
betray	cabriolet

AZE (see AISE)

CRE, CHRE (see ER)

E, EA (see EE)

EACE, EASE

cease	greasr
geese	fleece

lease	decease
niece	decrease
peace	increase
piece	release
apiece	surcease
caprice	frontispiece

EACH

beach	preach
bleach	reach
breach	teach
each	impeach
peach ''	

EAD (see EDE and EED)

EAF (see IEF)

EAGUE

league	intrigue
teague	renege
fatigue	

EAK, compare AKE

Words in eek may be allowed to pass as almost perfect rhymes with beak.

beak	peak
bleak	pique
cheek	reek
clique	seek
creak	sheik
creek	shriek
eke	sleek
freak	sneak
leak	speak
leek	squeak
meek	streak

teak	bezique
weak	bespeak
week	critique
wreak	oblique
antique	

EAL, EEL

deal	weal
deil	heal
eel	heel
feel	keel
leal	kneel
meal	wheal
peal	wheel
peel	zeal
reel	anneal
seal	appeal
squeal	conceal
steal	congeal
steel	repeal
teal	reveal
veal	

EALM—ELM

elm	whelm
helm	overwhelm
realm	

EALTH.

health	wealth
stealth	commonwealth

EAM—EEM

beam	gleam
bream	team
cream	teem
deem	theme
dream	beseem

blaspheme	seem		
esteem	stream		
ream	extreme		
scheme	misdeem		
scream	redeem		
seam	supreme		

EAMT—EMPT

dreamt	contempt
tempt	exempt
attempt	

EAN—EEN

Words in **een** may be allowed to pass as almost perfect rhymes to bean.

bean	guillotine
clean	intervene
dean	sheen
e'en	seen
glean	skein
green	spleen
keen	teen
lean	wean
mean	ween
mien	between
queen	canteen
screen	careen
demesne	convene
foreseen	demean
machine	margarine
obscene	nicotine
routine	quarantine
serene	submarine
unclean	tambourine
aniline	vaseline
crinoline	velveteen

EANT (see ENT)

EAP

cheap	sheep
creep	sleep
deep	steep
heap	sweep
keep	weep
neap	asleep
peep	beweep

EAR

beer	career
cheer	clear
deer	dear
ear	cohere
fear	compeer
fleer	endear
gear	revere
hear	severe
here	sincere
jeer	veneer
leer	auctioneer
mere	bandolier
near	buccaneer
peer	chandelier
queer	chanticleer
rear	chiffonier
sear	disappear
seer	domineer
sheer	engineer
smear	gondolier
sneer	hemisphere
spear	interfere
sphere	mountaineer
steer	muleteer
tier	musketeer
veer	mutineer
year	persevere
adhere	pioneer
appear	privateer
austere	charioteer
besmear	

EARCH (see ERCH)

EARD (see ERD)

EARL (see URL)

EARN (see ERN)

EART (see ART)

EARTH—ERTH

berth	earth
birth	mirth
dearth	worth

EAST

beast	least
east	priest
feast	

Also the preterites of verbs in **ease**; as ceas'd.

EAT, EET

Words in **eet** may be allowed to pass as almost perfect rhymes to beat.

beat	sheet
bleat	sleet
cheat	street
eat	sweet
feat	treat
feet	wheat
fleet	complete
greet	conceit
heat	concrete
meat	deceit
meet	defeat
mete	discreet
neat	discrete
seat	entreat

EAT, EET—Cont.

escheat	retreat
estreat	obsolete
replete	plebiscite

EATH, ETH

baith	wreath .
breath	underneath
heath	death
neath	faith
wraith	

And the archaic third person singular of verbs.

EATHE

breathe	wreathe
seethe	bequeathe
sheathe	

EAVE

cleave	bereave
eave	conceive
eve	deceive
grieve	unweave
heave	perceive
leave	receive
sleeve	relieve
thieve	reprieve
weave	disbelieve
achieve	interleave
aggrieve	interweave
believe	

EB, EBB

bleb	web
ebb	

ECK

beck	neck
check	peck
deck	spec
fleck	speck
geck	wreck

ECT

sect	project
affect	protect
aspect	reflect
collect	reject
correct	respect
deject	select
direct	subject
dissect	suspect
detect	architect
effect	circumspect
eject	disaffect
elect	disrespect
erect	indirect
expect	intellect
infect	incorrect
inspect	recollect
neglect	retrospect
object	

Also the preterites of verbs in eck; as henpeck'd.

ED

bed	red
bled	said
bread	shed
fed	shred
fled	sped
head	spread
lead	stead
read	thread

bred	behead
dead	homestead
dread	instead
tread	misled
wed	o'erspread
abed	

EDE (see EED)

EDGE, compare AGE, IDGE

edge	pledge
fledge	sedge
hedge	wedge
kedge	allege
ledge	knowledge

EE (see Y, second list)

bee	houri
flea	lessee
flee	on dit
free	rupeé
glee	trustee
gree	calipee
he	cap-a-pie
see	committee
she	coterie
spree	key
tea	knee
thee	lea
three	lee
tree	me
agree	nee
bawbee	plea
decree	sea
degree	devotee
foresee	disagree
fusee	filigree
grandee	jubilee

EE (see y, second list)—Cont.

jeu d'esprit	vis-a-vis
mortgagee	animalculae
nominee	con amore
peccavi	extempore
pedigree	felo de se
recipe	fac simile
referee	hyperbole
repartee	lapsus linguae
simile	sotto voce

Words ending in y short; as merry, symmetry.

EECE. (see EACE)

EECH (see EACH)

EED, EDE

bead	steed
bleed	weed
breed	concede
creed	decreed
deed	exceed
feed	impede
heed	indeed
knead	linseed
lead	precede
mead	proceed
meed	recede
need	succeed
plead	stampede
read	intercede
seed	supersede
speed	velocipede

EEF (see IEF)

EEK (see EAK)

EEL (see EAL)

EEM (see EAM)

EEN (see EAN)

EESE, EEZE

breeze	tease
cheese	these
ease	wheeze
freeze	appease
please	disease
seize	displease
sneeze	dives
squeeze	

Also the plurals of nouns in ee, ea; as fees, seas.

EET (see EAT)

EF (see IEF)

EFT

cleft	weft
left	bereft
theft	

EG

beg	peg
egg	seg
leg	philabeg
keg	

EGM (see EM)

EIGN (see AIN)

EIN (see AIN)

EINT (see AINT)

EIT (see EAT)

EL

bell	libel
belle	mongrel
cell	hell
dwell	knell
ell	mell
fell	quell
smell	sell
spell.	shell
swell	petrel
tell	rebel
well	repel
yell	sorrel
befell	towel
compel	vowel
dispel	yokel
excel	asphodel
expel	calomel
foretell	citadel
gazelle	doggerel
hotel	infidel
hovel	muscatel
impel	parallel
laurel	sentinel

ELD

eld	beheld
geld	upheld
held	withheld

Also-the preterites of verbs in ell; as swell'd.

ELF

delf	self
elf	shelf
pelf	himself

ELK

elk	whelk
kelk	

ELM (see EALM)

ELP

help	whelp
kelp	yelp

ELT

belt	melt
dealt	pelt
dwelt	smelt
felt	welt.
gelt	

ELVE

delve	shelve
helve	twelve

EM

gem	condemn
hem	contemn
kemb	anadem
phlegm	apothegm
stem	diadem
them	requiem
anthem	stratagem

EME (see EAM)

EMPT

dreamt	contempt
tempt	exempt
attempt	unkempt

den	acumen	eloquence	innocence
fen	citizen	eminence	indifference
hen	cozen	evidence	intelligence
ken	dozen	excellence	incontinence
men	foemen	frankincense	impenitence
pen	frozen	inference	impertinence
ten	hyphen	impotence	improvidence
then	omen	impudence	magnificence
wren	open	indigence	munificence
amen	oxen .	indolence	omnipotence
sharpen	seamen		
syren	semen		
vixen	denizen		
warden	oxygen		

ENCH

bench	tench
clench	trench
drench	wrench
quench	intrench
stench	retrench

ENCE, ENSE

cense	penitence	
dense	preference	
fence	providence	
hence	recompense	

END

pence	reference	bend	forefend
sense	residence	blend	impend
thence	reverence	end	misspend
whence	vehemence	friend	lend
commence	violence	tend	mend
condense	benevolence	vend	rend
defence	circumference	amend	send
dispense	concupiscence	ascend	spend
expense	silence	attend	offend
immense	suspense	befriend	obtend
incense	abstinence	commend	portend
intense	conference	contend	pretend
nonsense	confidence	defend	protend
offence	consequence	depend	suspend
pretence	continence	descend	transcend
prepense	difference	distend	unbend
prudence	diffidence	expend	apprehend
negligence	diligence	extend	comprehend

condescend	reprehend
dividend	reverend
recommend	

Also the preterites of verbs
in **en**; as kenn'd.

ENE (see EAN)

ENGE

avenge	revenge

ENGTH

length	strength

ENT

bent	extent
lent ·	ferment
pent	foment
meant	frequent
rent	indent
scent	intent
sent	invent
spent	condiment
tent	confident
vent	continent
went	corpulent
absent	detriment
ascent	different
assent	diligent
augment	discontent
cement	document
consent	element
content	eloquent
crescent	eminent
descent	evident
dissent	excellent

precedent	tournament	blur	martyr
president	turbulent	burr	master
prevalent	underwent	cur	miller
provident	vehement	err	miser
punishment	violent	purr	mitre
ravishment	virulent	sir.	murmur
redolent	accomplishment	slur	nadir
regiment	acknowledgment	spur	ogre
represent	admonishment	stir	oyster
resident	indifferent	whirr	pauper
reticent	incandescent	aver	forerunner
reverent	incompetent	barber	gardener
rudiment	incontinent	blister	grasshopper
sacrament	intelligent	brother	harbinger
sediment	irreverent	cadger	islander
sentiment	lineament	caper	lavender
settlement	magnificent	cipher	lawgiver
subsequent	malevolent	cloister	loiterer
succulent	mendicament	clover	lucifer
supplement	omnipotent	codger	mariner
tenement	temperament	coster	massacre
testament		cruiser	messenger
		dapper	minister
		daughter	murderer
ENTS (see ENCE)		dempster	officer
		deter	passenger
		differ	pillager
EP		douceur	presbyter
		foster	prisoner
nep	skep	ginger	provender
rep	demirep	heifer	register
step		hunger	reveller
		inter	sepulchre
		lawyer	slanderer
EPT		leather	sophister
		ledger	fir
crept	accept	leper	fur
kept	adept	lobster	her
sept	except	lover	myrrh
slept	intercept	lubber	pepper
wept			

pilfer	bespatter	
prefer	canister	
plunger	character	
rambler	chorister	
robber	conjurer	
rooster	cottager	
rover	cucumber	
scatter	cylinder	
simper	dowager	
singer	flatterer	
sinner	forager	
sister	foreigner	
skipper	sorcerer	
sloper	terrier	
smatter	theatre	
smuggler	thunderer	
soldier	traveller	
sombre	usurer	
spinster	villager	
stammer	victualler	
steamer	voyager	
stopper	waggoner	
stutter	wanderer	
summer	administer	
temper	adulterer	
toper	artificer	
trapper	astronomer	
transfer	astrologer	
trooper	filibuster	
whisper	idolater	
arbiter	interpreter	
armiger	philosopher	
barrister	amphitheatre	

Also the comparative of adjectives and nouns formed from verbs in **y;** as higher, buyer.

ERCE (see ERSE)

ERCH

church	search
lurch	smirch
perch	research

ERD

bird	herd
heard	sherd

Also' the preterites of verbs in **er, ur;** as err'd, purr'd.

ERF

scurf	surf
serf	turf

ERGE

dirge	diverge
merge	urge
purge	verge
scourge	emerge
serge	immerge
surge	

ERM

firm	affirm
term	confirm
worm	

ERN

burn	adjourn
churn	concern
dern	discern
earn	return
fern	learn
hern	quern
kerne	spurn
yearn	stern

90

ERVE

tern	sojourn	curve	disserve
turn	overturn	nerve	observe
urn		serve	preserve
		swerve	reserve
		conserve	subserve
		deserve	

ERSE

curse	coerce
hearse	converse
nurse	commerce
purse	disperse
terse	immerse
verse	perverse
worse	rehearse
accurse	reverse
adverse	traverse
amerce	intersperse
asperse	reimburse
averse	universe

ERT

blurt	dessert
curt	pert
dirt	shirt
flirt	skirt
hurt	spurt
vert	squirt
wert	divert
wort	exert
advert	expert
assert	inert
avert	insert
concert	invert
convert	pervert
culvert	subvert
desert	controvert

ERTH (see EARTH)

ES, ESS

bless	profess
cess	recess
chess	redress
cress	actress
dress	address
guess	artless
less	assess
mess	caress
press	compress
stress	confess
tress	congress
yes	countess
abbess	countless
abscess	depress
access	digress
duress	distress
express	duchess
excess	repress
fortress	sadness
fruitless	seamstress
gladness	sickness
guileless	spotless
guiltless	success
hopeless	tigress
impress	transgress
largess	acquiesce
madness	adultress
oppress	bashfulness
possess	coalesce
princess	effervesce

pennyless   foolhardiness

And numerous compounds in less and ness.

ESE (see EESE)

ESH

flesh	thresh
fresh	afresh
mesh	refresh

ESK

desk	moresque
burlesque	arabesque
grotesque	picturesque

EST

best	digest
breast	chest
guest	crest
jest	divest
lest	infest
nest	inquest
pest	invest
quest	molest
rest	obtest
test	protest
vest	request
west	suggest
abreast	unrest
arrest	interest
attest	manifest
bequest	overdrest
contest	palimpsest
detest	

Also the preterites of verbs in ess; as express'd.

bet
debt
fret
get
jet
let
met
net
set
sweat
threat
wet
whet
jet
abet
banquet
basket
beget
beset
blanket
bracelet
brunette
regret
rosette
roulette
sestet
serviette
signet
streamlet
target
ticket
toilet
triplet
upset
vignette
alphabet
amulet
anchoret
basinet
bayonet

ET, ETTE—Cont.

,violet	wagonette

ETCH

fetch	stretch
'sketch	wretch

ETH (see EATH)

ETE (see EAT)

EVE (see EAVE)

EUD (see UDE)

EUM (see UME)

EW, compare OO

cue	imbue
–dew	few
due	hew
Jew	hue
knew	nephew
mew	mildew
new	perdue
pew	purlieu
sue	pursue
view	renew
yew	review
adieu	statue
anew	subdue
askew	avenue
bedew	impromptu
bellevue	interview
curfew	parvenu
emew	residue
endue	retinue
ensue	revenue
eschew	

EX

sex	convex
vex	index
annex	perplex
apex	reflex
codex	vortex
complex	circumflex

Also the plurals of nouns and the preterites of verbs in **ecks**, as decks, recks.

EY (see AY)

I (see Y, first list)

IB

bib	nib
crib	rib
glib	squib

IBE

bribe	prescribe
scribe	proscribe
tribe	subscribe
ascribe	transcribe
describe	diatribe
imbibe	superscribe
inscribe	

IC (see ICK)

ICE, compare ISE

dice	slice
ice	vice
mice	advice
nice	concise
price	device

entice	splice
precise	rice
suffice	thrice
paradise	sacrifice
spice	

ICH (see ITCH)

ICK

brick	artistic
chick	bucolic
kick	prognostic
lick	quixotic
nick	realistic
pick	rhetoric
quick	romantic
sick	schismatic
stick	splenetic
thick	antiseptic
tick	antagonistic
trick	arithmetic
attic	beatific
arctic	cabalistic
antic	catholic
caustic	choleric
chronic	didactic
colic	dogmatic
comic	domestic
critic	dramatic
cynic	electric
drastic	emetic
hectic	emphatic
physic	erratic
picnic	euphonic
plastic	exotic
rustic	forensic
acrostic	heretic
agnostic	iambic
aquatic	fantastic

lunatic	poetic
lymphatic	politic
magnetic	prophetic
majestic	dyspeptic
mechanic	eccentric
mimetic	epidemic
memphitic	hieroglyphic
narcotic	idiomatic
nomadic	morganatic
pacific	paleocrystic
pathetic	panegyric
phlegmatic	peripatetic
plethoric	prognostic

ICT

strict	conflict
addict	inflict
afflict	relict
convict	contradict

Also the preterites of verbs in ick; as kick'd.

ID

bid	eyelid
chid	florid
grid	foetid
hid	forbid
kid	frigid
lid	hybrid
quid	morbid
rid	orchid
slid	placid
aquid	rabid
acid	solid
amid	sordid
arid	torpid
bestrid	turgid

Also the preterites of verbs in ry; as married, buried.

IDE

bide	beside
bride	bestride
chide	collide
glide	confide
guide	decide
hide	deride
pride	divide
ride	misguide
side	preside
slide	provide
stride	reside
tide	subside
wide	parricide
abide	regicide
aside	subdivide
astride	suicide
betide	infanticide

Also the preterites of verbs in **ie, y;** as died, defied, and sigh'd.

IDES

ides	besides

Also the plurals of nouns and the preterites of verbs in **ide;** as tides, rides.

IDGE, compare AGE

bridge	college
fidge	steerage
midge	privilege
ridge	sacrilege
abridge	

IDST

didst	amidst
midst	

Also the second person singular of verbs in **id;** as bidd'st.

IE (see Y)

IEF

beef	sheaf
brief	reef
chief	thief
fief	belief
grief	relief
lief	

IEGE

liege	assiege
siege	besiege

IELD

field	wield
shield	yield
weald	afield

Also the preterites of verbs in **eel;** as wheel'd.

IEN (see EAN)

IEND (see END)

IERCE (see SREE)

IES (see IS, ISE)

IEST (see EAST)

IEVE (see EAVE)

IF, IFF

cliff	whiff
skiff	caitiff
sniff	caliph
stiff	dandriff
tiff	midwife

plaintiff	hieroglyph
sheriff	

IFE

fife	rife
knife	strife
life	wife

IFT

drift	whiff't
gift	rift
lift	shift
sift	adrift
thrift	snowdrift
tiff'd	spendthrift

IG

big	rig
dig	snig
fig	sprig
gig	swig
grig	twig
jig	whig
pig	wig
prig	whirligig

IGE

oblige (no rhyme)

IGH (see Y, first list)

IGHT (see ITE)

IGN (see INE)

IGUE (see EAGUE)

IKE

dike	alike
glike	like
shrike	pike
spike	dislike
strike	

ILD

child	wild
mild	

Also the preterites of verbs in ile; as smil'd, revil'd.

ILE

aisle	reconcile
bile	tile
chyle	vile
file	while
guile	awhile
isle	beguile
mile	compile
pile	defile
smile	edile
stile	erewhile
style	exile
pensile	gentile
revile	bibliophile
crocodile	

ILL, compare ILE

bill	ill
chill	kill
drill	mill
fill	pill
frill	quill
gill	rill
grill	shrill
hill	skill

ILL, compare ILE—Com.

spill	instil
still	missile
swill	pencil
thrill	peril
till	Sibyl
trill	codicil
will	daffodil
distil	deshabille
fulfil	utensil
idyll	

Also many words in **ile** accented on the penultimate or antepenultimate syllable; as fertile, juvenile.

ILK

milk	silk

ILT

built	hilt
gilt	jilt
guilt	milt
quilt	stilt
spilt	tilt

ILTH

filth	tilth

IM

brim	rim
dim	skim
grim	slim
him	trim
hymn	whim
limb	pilgrim
limn	pseudonym
prim	synonym

IME

chime	rhyme
climb	slime
clime	time
crime	thyme
grime	sublime
lime	maritime
prime	overtime

IMES

betimes	sometimes

Also the plurals of nouns and the third person singular of verbs in **ime**; as times, rhymes.

IMP

gimp	limp
imp	pimp
jimp	

IMPSE

glimpse	limps

IN, compare INE

bin	spin
chin	thin
din	tin
fin	twin
gin	whin
grin	win
inn	akin
kin	begin
lin	buskin
pin	chagrin
shin	codlin
sin	griffin
skin	margin

maudlin	welkin
muffin	cannakin
raisin	javelin
ruin	kilderkin
sanguine	mandolin
satin	manikin
tiffin	origin
tocsin	palanquin
virgin	violin
urchin	

INCE

mince	since
prince	wince
quince	convince
rinse	evince

INCH

clinch	pinch
finch	winch
inch	

INCT

link'd	instinct
tinct	precinct
distinct	succinct
extinct	

IND

bind	rind
blind	wind
find	behind
grind	remind
kind	unkind
mind	

Also the preterites of verbs in ine; as twin'd.

brine	design
chine	divine
fine	enshrine
kine	dine
lince	entwine
min	incline
nine	indign
pine	opine
shine	recline
sign	refine
sine	repine
shrine	saline
syne	supine
thine	akaline
trine	brigantine
twine	columbine
vine	concubine
whine	countermine
wine	crystalline
assign	incarnadine
combine	interline
condign	leonine
confine	porcupine
consign	superfine
decline	turpentine
define	undermine

There is no certain rule as to the letter i in the suffix ine being long or short, but in either case words so ending form passable rhymes. It is long in feline, confine, crystalline, turpentine, etc.; short in genuine, heroine, jessamine, medicine, etc.; in such words as alkaline, uterine, custom is unsettled.

ING

bring	ging
cling	fling

king	thing	
ring	wing	
sing	wring	
sling	darling	
spring	foundling	
sting	startling	
suckling	sterling	
yearling	stripling	
string	underling	
swing		

Also the present participles of verbs, and participal adjectives in ing; as drinking, laughing.

INGE

cringe	tinge
dinge	twinge
fringe	lozenge
hinge	infringe
singe	orange
springe	syringe
swinge	

INK

blink	sink
brink	skink
chink	slink
clink	stink
drink	swink
ink	think
link	wink
pink	zinc
rink	bethink
shrink	forethink

INT

dint	quint
flint	squint
hint	tint
lint	asquint
mint	imprint
print	

INTH

absinthe	hyacinth
plinth	labyrinth

INX

jinks	sphinx
minx	

IP

chip	trip
clip	whip
dip	courtship
drip	cowslip
hip	equip
lip	friendship
nip	gossip
rip	hardship
pip	horsewhip
scrip	landslip
ship	township
sip	tulip
skip	turnip
slip	worship
snip	fellowship
strip	workmanship
tip	

IPE

gripe	ripe
pipe	snipe

stripe	archetype
type	prototype
wipe	stereotype

IPSE

Eclipse—rhymes with the plurals of nouns, and the third person singular of verbs in ip; as nips, clips.

IQUE (see EAK)

IR (see ER)

IRCH (see URCH)

IRD (see URD)

IRE, compare AR, ER

dire	admire
fire	aspire
gyre	attire
hire	conspire
ire	desire
lyre	entire
mire	expire
pyre	inspire
quire	inquire
sire	require
spire	retire
squire	satire
tire	transpire
wire	umpire
acquire	

IRGE (see ERGE)

IRK

burke	firk
dirk	jerk

kirk	smirk
lurk	stirk
murk	work

IRL (see URL)

IRM

chirm	affirm
firm	confirm
term	infirm
worm	

IRST (see URST)

IRT (see ERT)

IRTH

birth	mirth
dearth	worth
earth	

IS, IZ

his	whiz
fizz	breeches
phiz	

Also the plurals of ma nouns in cy, sy; as mercies.

ISS

bliss	axis
hiss	chalice
kiss	crisis
miss	dais
spiss	dismiss
this	gratis
wis	jaundice
abyss	lattice
amis	lettuce

notice	prejudice
novice	prolapsis
phthisis	synthesis
remiss	verdigris
service	amanuensis
thesis	aposiopesis
analysis	diagnosis
antithesis	metamorphosis
artifice	metempsychosis
chrysalis	metropolis
emphasis	necropolis
paralysis	parenthesis

ISE, compare ICE

guise	enterprise
prize	advise
rise	assize
size	chastise
wise	comprise
devise	despise
disguise	exercise
excise	idolise
premise	pulverise
revise	realise
supplies	improvise
surmise	sacrifise
surprise	signalise
agonise	solemnise
authorise	summarise
canonise	sympathise
catechise	tyrannise
circumcise	immortalise
civilize	systematise
criticise	

Also the third person singular of verbs in **y**; as cries,
tries.

ISH

dish	pish
fish	banish

cherish	radish
finish	relish
flourish	squeamish
nourish	rubbish
parish	astonish
perish	demolish

ISK

brisk	basilisk
disc	obelisk
frisk	odalisque
risk	tamarisk
whisk	

ISM

chrism	mysticism
prism	nepotism
schism	organism
abysm	occultism
altruism	optimism
baptism	pantheism
deism	pessimism
theism	plagiarism
truism	radicalism
aphorism	realism
barbarism	socialism
cataclysm	solecism
criticism	stoicism
egotism	syllogism
euphemism	vandalism
euphuism	vulgarism
heroism	witticism
hypnotism	anachronism
mesmerism	malthusianism

ISP

crisp	wisp
lisp	

IST

fist	optimist
list	organist
mist	chemist
twist	consist
whist	desist
wrist	dentist
assist	exist
artist	insist
persist	linquist
resist	papist
sophist	pessimist
subsist	pianist
alchemist	pugilist
amethyst	rhapsodist
annalist	ritualist
analyst	satirist
bigamist	socialist
dogmatist	vocalist
eucharist	anatomist
exorcist	antagonist
herbalist	diplomatist
humourist	evangelist
oculist	rationalist

Also the preterites of verbs in **iss**; as hiss'd.

IT

bit	twit
cit	whit
chit	wit
fit	writ
flit	acquit
grit	admit
hit	biscuit
knit	bowsprit
pit	commit
quit	emit
sit	forfeit
split	hermit

minute
omit
outwit
orbit
permit
pewit
rabbit

IT—Cont.

refit,
remit
submit
transmit
benefit
jesuit
perquisite

ITCH

bitch	rich
ditch	twitch
hitch	fitch
itch	flitch
niche	which
stitch	witch
switch	bewitch
pitch	enrich

ITE

bite	incite
blight	indict
bright	indite
cite	invite
fight	midnight
flight	moonlight
fright	polite
height	recite
kite	requite
knight	twilight
light	unite
mite	upright
night	zoophite
pight	aconite
plight	acolyte
quite	anchorite
right	slight
rite	smite
sight	spite

sprite	despite
tight	excite
trite	foresight
white	disunite
wight	appetite
write	dynamite
accite	expedite
affright	oversight
alight	parasite
aright	proselyte
bedight	reunite
benight	satellite
contrite	stalactite
delight	sybarite

ITH

frith	sith
kith	smith
pith	zenith

ITHE

blithe	scythe
hithe	tithe
lithe	writhe

IVE (as in dive)

dive	five
drive	gyve
hive	connive
rive	contrive
shrive	deprive
strive	derive
thrive	revive
alive	survive
arrive	

IVE

give	sieve
live	active

forgive	punitive
furtive	purgative
massive	relative
motive	sensitive
native	subjective
outlive	talkative
passive	affirmative
pensive	contemplative
restive	demonstrative
suasive	diminutive
votive	distributive
fugitive	imaginative
laxative	inquisitive
narrative	prerogative
objective	submissive
perspective	restorative
positive	

IX

fix	onyx
six	prefix
mix	statics
nix	transfix
affix	crucifix
matrix	intermix
mechanics	mathematics
hydrostatics	rheumatics

Also the plurals of nouns in **icks;** as bricks.

IZE (see ISE)

O

ago	go
beau	hoe
dough	lo
foe	mo
fro	no

O—Cont.

oh.	stingo
roe	zero
sloe	apropos
though	calico
throe	camco
woe	comme il faut
banjo	domino
bureau	de novo
chapeau	embryo
chateau	falsetto
cocoa	fandango
dado	folio
depot	indigo
echo	in petto
grotto	libretto
gusto	mistletoe
negro	mulatto
stilletto	octavo
tobacco	piano
tomato	portmanteau
tornado	sirocco
torpedo	soprano
virago	braggadocio
volcano	imbroglio
adagio	magnifico
duodecimo	innuendo
photo	oratorio
plateau	peccadillo
polo	seraglio
quarto	generalissimo
rondeau	quid pro que
solo	

OACH

broach	abroach
brooch	approach
coach	encroach
loach	reproach
poach	

OAD (see ODE)

OAF (see OFF)

OAK (see OKE)

OAL (see OLE)

OAM (see OME)

OAN (see ONE)

OAP (see OPE)

OAR (see ORE)

OARD (see ORD)

OAST (see OST)

OAT (see OTE)

OATH (see OTH)

OB

bob	rob
cob	sob
fob	squab
hob	swab
lob	throb
knob	cabob
mob	hobnob
nob	nabob

OBE

globe	robe
lobe	conglobe
probe	

OCE (see OSE)

OCK

block	cock
brock	clock

OCK—Cont.

crock
dock
flock
frock
hough
knock
lock
lough
mock
shock
sock
stock

toque
rock
bannock
bullock
havoc
haycock
hillock
padlock
peacock
pibroch
shamrock

OCT

decoct   concoct

Also the preterites of verbs in ock; as shock'd.

OD

cod
clod
God
hod
nod
odd
plod
pod

quad
quod
rod
shod
sod
tod
trod
wad

ODE

bode
code
goad
load
mode
node
ode
road
rode
toad

woad
abode
commode
corrode
explode
forebode
a'-la-mode
episode
incommode

ODGE

bodge
dodge

lodge
podge

OFF

cough
doff
off

scoff
trough

OFT

croft
cough'd
oft

soft
scoff'd
aloft

OG, OGUE

bog
clog
cog
dog
hog
fog
frog
jog
log
prog

shog
agog
prologue
catalogue
demagogue
dialogue
epilogue
pedagogue
synagogue

OICE, compare OISE

choice
voice

rejoice

OID

void
avoid
devoid
asteroid

alkaloid
amyloid
cycloid
spheroid

Also the preterites of verbs in oy; as buoy'd.

OIL

boil	spoil
coil	toil
foil	despoil
moil	embroil
oil	recoil
soil	turmoil

OIN

coin	subjoin
foin	sirloin
groin	proin
join	quoin
loin	adjoin
purloin	disjoin
rejoin	enjoin

OINT

joint	appoint
oint	disjoint
point	counterpoint
anoint	disappoint

OISE, compare OICE

noise	counterpoise
poise	equipoise

Also the plurals of nouns, and the preterites of verbs in oy; as toys, employs.

OIST

foist	moist
hoist	rejoic'd

OIT

coit	exploit
quoit	dacoit
adroit	

OKE

broke	spoke
cloak	stroke
croak	yoke
folk	yolk
joke	awoke
oak	bespoke
poke	invoke
smoke	revoke
soak	artichoke

OL

doll	extol
loll	alcohol
poll	capitol
carol	

OLD

bold	behold
cold	cuckold
fold	enfold
gold	foretold
hold	freehold
mould	unfold
old	uphold
scold	withhold
sold	manifold
told	marigold
wold	

Also the preterites of verbs in oll, ole, owl; as roll'd, bowl'd.

OLE, compare OWL

bole	goal
coal	hole
dole	jole
droll	mole
foal	pole

OLE, compare OWL—Cont.

role	console
shoal	creole
sole	parole
stole	pistole
whole	aureole
cajole	girandole
condole	girasole

OLN

stol'n	swol'n

OLT

bolt	holt
colt	moult
dolt	thunderbolt

OLVE

solve	involve
absolve	resolve
convolve	revolve
dissolve	

OM (see UM)

OMB (see OOM)

dome	mome
foam	roam
home	tome
loam	

OMP

pomp	swamp
romp	

ON, compare UN

con	swan
don	anon
gone	arson

ON, compare UN—Cont.

bonbon	parson
canon	poison
cannon	prison
colon	reason
felon	season
iron	squadron
lemon	tendon
jargon	amazon
mammon	battalion
horizon	cinnamon
lexicon	clarion
million	dies non
myrmidon	environ
orison	halcyon
pro et con	criterion
simpleton	diapason
automaton	phenomenon
pardon	sine qua non

ONCE (see UNCE)

OND

bond	beyond
conn'd	despond
donn'd	second
fond	correspond
pond	diamond
abscond	vagabond
almond	

ONE, compare OWN

bone	dethrone
cone	enthrone
drone	postpone
groan	monotone
hone	telephone
loan	moan
lone	prone
atone	stone

ONE, compare OWN—Cont.

tone	alone
throne	undertone .
zone	

ONG

long	along
prong	among
song	belong
strong	ding-dong
thong	prolong
throng	bon-vivant
wrong	

ONK (see UNK)

ONSE (see UNCE)

ONT, compare UNT

ont	want

OO, compare EW

blew	you
blue	accrue
brew	ado
chew	bamboo
clue	bas-blue
coo	canoe
lew	crew
loo	drew
pooh	glue
rue	grew
screw	coup
shrew	fou
slew	canoe
threw	cuckoo
through	debut
too	imbrue
true	shampoo
two	skidoo
who	taboo
woo	tattoo

OO, compare EW—Cont.

undo	billet-doux
waterloo	entre nous
withdrew	cockatoo
yahoo	kangaroo

OOD, compare UD. UDE

brood	mood
brew'd	rude
coo'd	woo'd
food	

OOF

hoof	aloof
proof	behoof
roof	disproof
wdof	reproof

OOK, compare UCK

book	rook
brook	shook
cook	took
crook	betook
fluke	forsook
hook	mistook
look	undertook

OOL, compare ULE

buhl	spool
cool	stool
fool	tool
pool	befool
rule	cesspool
school	

OOM, compare UME

bloom	gloom
doom	groom

loom	tomb
plume	whom
rheum	womb
room	entomb
spoom	

OON, compare UNE

boon	lampoon
croon	monsoon
moon	noon
soon	prune
spoon	poltroon
swoon	pontoon
balloon	quadroon
basoon	shalloon
buffoon	simoon
cartoon	typhoon
cocoon	honeymoon
dragoon	octoroon
festoon	pantaloon
lagoon	

OOP

coop	sloop
droop	soup
group	stoop
hoop	stoup
loop	troop
poop	whoop
scoop	nincompoop

OOR, compare ORE, URE

boor	your
moor	amour
poor	contour
sure	detour
tour	paramour

OOSE (see UCE)

OOT, compare UTE

boot	moot
coot	root
flute	shoot
hoot	cheroot
loot	uproot

OOTH

booth	soothe
smooth	

OOVE (see OVE)

OOZE (see USE)

OP

chop	trollop
crop	prop
drop	shop
flop	slop
fop	strop
hop	sop
mop	stop
pop	swop
bishop	top
collop	develop
gallop	envelop
scallop	

OPE

cope	aslope
hope	elope
grope	antelope
mope	envelope
ope	heliotrope
pope	horoscope
rope	interlope
soap	kaleidoscope
scope	microscope
slope	misanthrope
trope	telescope

OR, compare ER, ORE

corps	counsellor
tor	emperor
war	governor
abhor	flavour
anchor	horror
author	honour
doctor	labour
donor	mirror
hector	motor
sculptor	parlour
stupor	prior
suitor	sailor
tailor	metaphor
tenor	orator
traitor	savior
tutor	senator
vendor	warrior
victor	alligator
ancestor	ambassador
auditor	competitor
bachelor	conspirator
chancellor	excelsior
conqueror	progenitor
creator	solicitor
creditor	

ORCE (see ORSE)

ORCH

porch	torch
scorch	

ORD

board	sword
cord	abhorr'd
ford	aboard
hoard	accord
horde	afford
lord	implor'd
roar'd	record

ORE, compare OOR

ORE

boar	whore
bore	wore
floor	yore
four	core
gore	door
lore	adore
more	afore
oar	ashore
o'er	claymore
ore	deplore
pore	encore
pour	explore
roar	forebore
score	foreswore
shore	implore
snore	restore
soar	albicore
sore	hellebore
store	heretofore
swore	sycamore
tore	troubadour

ORGE

forge	disgorge
gorge	regorge

ORK, compare ALK

cork	pork
fork	stork
ork	

ORM

form	reform
storm	transform
conform	misinform
deform	multiform
inform	uniform
perform	

ORN, compare AWN

born	adorn
borne	foreborne
corn	foresworn
horn	forlorn
lorn	lovelorn
morn	suborn
scorn	capricorn
shorn	chloroform
sorn	multiform
sworn	overborne
thorn	thunderstorm
torn	unicorn
worn	uniform

ORSE, ORCE

coarse	morse
corse	torse
course	endorse
force	remorse
horse	unhorse .

ORT, compare OUGHT

court	wart
fort	cohort
mort	consort
port	distort
short	exhort
snort	extort
sort	report
tort	resort
retort	

ORTH

forth	north
fourth	

OS (see OSS)

OSE, OZE

chose	disclose
close (verb)	dispose
doze	enclose
foes	expose
froze	foreclose
goes	impose
hose	oppose
nose	propose
pose	repose
prose	suppose
rose	transpose
those	discompose
toes	interpose
arose	presuppose
compose	recompose
depose	

OSS

boss	chaos
cross	emboss
loss	doss
moss	dross
across	albatross
bathos	asbestos

OST

cost	accost
frost	holocaust
lost	exhaust
toss'd	

OT

blot	knot
clot	lot
cot	trot
got	yacht
grot	allot
hot	ballot
jot	bigot

OT—Cont.

boycot	shot
complot	sot
forgot	spot
apricot	squat
not	counterplot
plot	idiot
pot	melilot
quat	polyglot
rot	

OTCH

blotch	notch
botch	watch
crotch	

OTE

bloat	remote
boat	anecdote
coat	mote
float	note
goat	quote
gloat	rote
groat	smote
lote	throat
moat	tote
afloat	vote
denote	wrote
devote	antidote
lifeboat	asymptote
misquote	petticoat
promote	table d'hote

OTH

broth	sloth
cloth	troth
froth	wrath
moth	

OTHE (see OOTH)

clothe	loathe

OU (see OO and OW)

OUCH

couch	slouch
crouch	vouch
ouch	avouch
pouch	barouche

OUD

cloud	aloud
crowd	enshroud
loud	o'ercloud
proud	o'ershroud
shroud	

Also the preterites of some verbs in ow; as how'd.

OUGH

This much abused combination of letters—the terror of foreigners who try to speak our tongue—has no fewer than nine different sounds, as enumerated below.

cough as in off

chough ⎫
rough |
slough ⎬ as in stuff.
sough |
tough ⎭

bough ⎱ as in cow.
plough ⎰

hough ⎱ as in lock.
lough ⎰

hiccough as in cup
slough as in slow
through as in too

dough ⎱ as in toe
though ⎰

ought ⎱ as in awe.
thought ⎰

OUGHT, compare ORT

aught	sought
bought	taught
brought	thought
caught	wrought
fought	besought
fraught	bethought
naught	forethought
nought	methought
ought	

OUL (see OLE, OWL)

OULD (see OLD, UD)

OUNCE

bounce	ounce
flounce	pounce
denounce	renounce
pronounce	

OUND

bound	aground
found	around
frown'd	compound
ground	confound
hound	expound
mound	profound
pound	propound
round	rebound
sound	resound
wound(to wind)	surround
abound	

OUNT

count	discount
fount	dismount
mount	miscount
account	remount
amount	surmount

OUP (see OOP)

OUR, compare OOR, ORE

bower	power
dower	scour
cower	sour
flour	tower
hour	deflower
lour	devour

OURN (see ORN, URN)

OURS

ours

The plurals of nouns and the third person singular of verbs in our, ower; as hours, towers, devours.

OURSE (see ORSE)

OUS (see US)

OUSE, compare OWSE

chouse	house
dowse	louse
grouse	mouse

OUT

bout	spout
clout	sprout
doubt	stout
drought	tout
gout	trout
grout	about
out	devout
pout	misdoubt
rout	redoubt
scout	throughout
shout	without
snout	

drought   south
mouth

(The verb which has no rhyme.)

OVE

As in love

dove   shove
glove   above
love

As in prove

move   disprove
groove   disapprove
prove   improve
approve   reprove

As in wove

clove   strove
drove   throve
grove   wove
hove   alcove
rove   behove
stove   interwove

OW, compare OO

AS in low

blow   show
bow   slough
crow   slow
flow   snow
glow   stow
grow   strow
know   throw
low   trow
mow   below
owe   bestow
row   billow
sew   callow
sow   fallow

OW, compare OO—

As in low.

foreknow   window
pillow   winnow
sallow   yellow
shallow   outgrow
swallow   overflow
wallow   overthrow
willow

As in now

bough   brow
cow   sow
frau   thou
how   vow
now   allow
plough   avow
prow   endow
row   disallow

OWL, compare OLE

The sounds of **owl** in **bowl** and **howl**, and of **ole** in **hole** are so similar as to be allowed to pass as almost **perfect** rhymes.

bowl   roll
cowl   scowl
fowl   soul
ghoul   toll
growl   troll
howl   control
owl   enroll
poll   patrol
prowl

OWN, compare ONE

The sounds of **own** in **blown** and **frown**, and of **one** in **stone** are so similar as to be al-

lowed to pass as almost perfect rhymes.

blown	noun
brown	own
clown	shown
crown	strewn
down	thrown
drown	town
frown	adown
gown	embrown
mown	renown

OWSE

browse	touse
house (verb)	trouse
rouse	carouse
spouse	espouse

Also the plurals of some
nouns, and the third person
singular of verbs in ow; as
brows, allows.

OX

box	orthodox
fox	paradox
ox	heterodox
equinox	

Also the plurals of nouns,
and the third person singular
of verbs in ock; as cocks,
mocks.

OY

boy	annoy
buoy	convoy
cloy	decoy
coy	destroy
joy	employ
toy	enjoy
alloy	sepoy

OZE (see OSE)

U (see EW)

UB

chub	rub
club	shrub
cub	slub
drub	snub
dub	tub
grub	hubbub
hub	beelzebub

UBE

cube	rube
tube	jujube

UCE

deuce	disuse (noun)
goose	excuse
juice	induce
moose	misuse
puce	obtuse
sluice	produce
spruce	propose
truce	recluse
use (noun)	reduce
abuse	seduce
obstruse	traduce
conduse	introduce
deduce	

UCH

crutch	such
much	touch
hutch	retouch

UCK

buck	struck
duck	suck
luck	truck
muck	tuck
pluck	

UCT

suck'd	instruct
conduct	obstruct
duck'd	aqueduct
deduct	viaduct

UD

blood	stood
bud	stud
could	rud
cud	wood
flood	would
good	brotherhood
hood	likelihood
mud	neighborhood
scud	understood
should	widowhood

UDE, compare UD

brood	exude
crude	include
feud	intrude
jewed	obtrude
lewd	rrotrude
snood	seclude
allude	altitude
conclude	aptitude
delude	attitude
elude	fortitude
exclude	gratitude

UDE, compare UD—Cont.

habitude	platitude
interlude	plenitude
prude	promptitude
nude	servitude
rood	solitude
rude	beatitude
lassitude	ingratitude
latitude	inaptitude
longitude	similitude
magnitude	solicitude
multitude	vicissitude

Also the preterites of som
verbs in ew; as view'd.

UDGE

budge	sludge
drudge	smudge
fudge	trudge
grudge	adjudge
judge	prejudge
nudge	

UE (see EW, OO)

UFF

bluff	counterbuff
buff	rough
chough	ruff
chuff	slough
cuff	snuff
gruff	stuff
huff	tough
luff	enough
puff	rebuff

UG

drug	hug
dug	jug

UG—Cont.

mug	slug	bulk	ULK
pug	snug	hulk	skulk
rug	tug		sulk
shrug	humbug		

UICE (see OOSE)

ULP

gulp   sculp
pulp

UISE (see ISE. OOZE)

UIT (see UTE

pulse   impulse
convulse   repulse
expulse

UKE

duke	chibouque
fluke	rebuke
puke	

ULT

cult	insult
adult	occult
consult	result
exult	catapult
indult	difficult

UL, ULL

bull	bashful
cull	brimful
dull	careful
full	dreadful
gull	faithful
hull	grateful
lull	thoughtful
mull	beautiful
null	bountiful
pull	dutiful
skull	fanciful
trull	merciful
wool	sorrowful
annul	wonderful
awful	worshipful

UM

chum	laudanum
come	phantom
crum	succumb
crumb	winsome
drum	asylum
dumb	burdensome
plum	cumbersome
scum	frolicsome.
slum	humoursome
sum	mausoleum
swum	maximum
thrum	glum
thumb	gum
become	hum
gruesome	mum
gypsum	numb
handsome	millennium
hansom	minimum
humdrum	opium

ULE, compare OOL

mule	reticule
pule	redicule
yule	vestibule
ferule	

ULGE

bulge	indulge
divulge	

UM—Cont.

overcome	encomium
pendulum	interregnum
quarrelsome	memorandum
solatium	opprobrium
troublesome	palladium
auditorium	pandemonium
crematorium	residuum
delirium ·	symposium
gymnasium	

UME, compare OOM

fume	perfume
plume	presume
assume	resume
consume	volume
deplume	

UMP

bump	frump
clump	jump
lump	stump
plump	thump
pump	trump
rump	

UN, compare ON

done	ton
dun	tun
gun	won
none	begun
nun	boatswain
one	coxswain
pun	undone
run	comparison
shun	garrison
son	onion
spun	skeleton
stun	union
sun	

UNCE

unce	once

UNCH

bunch	munch
crunch	punch
hunch	scrunch
lunch	

UND

fund	refund
shunn'd	moribund
stunn'd	

UNE, compare OON

hewn	untune
tune	importune
jejune	

UNG

bung	stung
clung	sung
dung	swung
flung	tongue
hung	wrung
rung	young
slung	among
sprung	unsung
strung	

UNGE

lunge	sponge
plunge	expunge

UNK

bunk	shrunk
chunk	skunk
drunk	slunk
hunk	stunk
junk	sunk
monk	trunk
punk	

UNT

blunt	grunt
brunt	hunt
front	wont

UP

cup	hiccough
pup	stirrup
sup	syrup

UPT

abrupt	supp'd
corrupt	interrupt

UR (see ER)

URB

curb	disturb
herb	suburb
verb	

URCH (see ERCH)

URD

bird	word
curd	absurd
gird	referr'd
stirr'd	

URE

cure	obscure
dure	ordure
ewer	procure
lure	secure
pure	calenture
brochure	coverture
conjure	skewer
demure	abjure
endure	adjure
immure	allure
inure	azure
manure	epicure
mature	forfeiture

URE—Cont.

immature	sinecure
miniature	investiture
overture	temperature
portraiture	primogeniture

URF

scurf	surf
serf	turf

URGE (see ERGE)

URK (see IRK)

URL

churl	earl
curl	furl
girl	twirl
hurl	uncurl
pearl	unfurl

URLD

world

The preterites of verbs in url; as furl'd, hurl'd.

URN (see ERN)

URP

chirp	extirp
discerp	usurp

URSE (see ERSE)

URST

burst	worst
curst	accurst
durst	vers'd
first	dispers'd
thirst	immers'd

URT (see ERT)

US, OUS

buss	glorious
hus	tyrannous
thus	valorous
truss	venomous
us	vigorous
bulbous	villainous
bumptious	adventurous
callous	adulteress
caucus	ambiguous
cautious	calamitous
circus	cadaverous
crocus	calcareous
discuss	cantankerous
focus	diaphanous
gracious	fortuitous
grievous	gratuitous
heinous	harmonious
litmus	hilarious
mucus	hocus-pocus
nervous	idolatrous
nimbus	ignis fatuus
pious	impecunious
porous	impetuous
rebus	ignoramus
vicious	incredulous
amorous	glutinous
arquebus	gluttonous
bibulous	hazardous
blasphemous	hideous
boisterous	humorous
clamorous	impetuous
credulous	incubus
curious	infamous
dangerous	lecherous
delicious	libellous
dolorous	litigious
emulous	luminous
fabulous	marvellous
frivolous	mischievous
garrulous	mountainous
generous	mutinous

US, OUS—Cont.

numerous	timorous
odious	traitorous
odorous	treacherous
ominous	indigenous
omnibus	libidinous
overplus	oleaginous
perilous	magnanimous
poisonous	miraculous
ponderous	necessitous
populous	obstreperous
prosperous	odoriferous
pugnacious	omnivorous
ravenous	pachydermatous
rigorous	ridiculous
riotous	solicitous
ruinous	somniferous
scandalous	thaumaturgus
scrupulous	victorious
sedulous	viviparous
serious	vociferous
slanderous	ubiquitous
sonorous	unanimous
stimulous	ungenerous

USE

booze	accuse
bruise	amuse
choose	diffuse
lose	disuse (verb)
muse	excuse
noose	infuse
ooze	misuse
ruse	peruse
shoes	refuse
use (verb)	suffuse
abuse	transfuse

Also the plurals of nouns and the third person singular of verbs in ew and uc; as dews, sues.

USH

blush	hush
brush	lush
bush	push
crush	rush
flush	thrush
frush	tush
gush	

USK

brusque	musk
lusk	tusk
husk	

UST

bust	discuss'd
crust	disgust
dust	distrust
just	focuss'd
lust	locust
must	intrust
rust	mistrust
thrust	rubust
trust	unjust
adjust	

UT

butt	slut
cut	smut
glut	soot
gut	strut
hut	abut
jut	gamut
nut	catgut
rut	englut
scut	rebut
shut	walnut

UTCH

clutch	hutch
crutch	much

UTCH—Cont.

such	retouch
touch	

UTE, compare OOT

bruit	recruit
brute	refute
cute	repute
flute	salute
fruit	absolute
lute	attribute
mute	constitute
newt	contribute
suit	destitute
acute	dissolute
compute	execute
confute	institute
depute	parachute
dilute	persecute
dispute	prosecute
impute	resolute
minute	substitute
pollute	

UX

crux	lux
dux	reflux
flux	

Also the plurals of nouns and the third person singular of verbs in uck; as trucks, sucks.

Y

As an end letter y has two sounds, the long i as in mile, and the short i, as in mill, the former rhyming perfectly with such words as die, sigh, the latter allowably with he, see, etc. Both, however, are used indiscriminately by all our poets; but for convenience' sake, lists of words of the two sounds are given separately.

Y long as in eye.

ay	fortify
buy	fructify
cry	gratify
die	glorify
dry	horrify
eye	justify
fie	magnify
fry	modify
hie	mollify
high	sigh
lie	sky
nigh	sly
pie	spy
ply	sty
pry	thigh
rye	tie
defy	try
deny	vie
descry	why
imply	ally
espy	apply
outvie	awry
outfly	belie
rely	comply
reply	decry
supply	mortify
untie	multiply
amplify	pacify
beautify	petrify
certify	prophesy
crucify	purify
deify	puterfy
dignify	qualify
edify	ramify
falsify	rarefy

ratify	terrify
rectify	testify
sanctify	verify
satisfy	villify
scarify	vivify
signify	indemnify
simplify	intensify
specify	lullaby
stupefy	solidify

Y short, as ty in duty.

beauty	happy
bonnie	haughty
brandy	hearty
busy	heavy
comely	homely
cosy	honey
crazy	hourly
crusty	humbly
curly	hungry
daily	hurry
dainty	jaunty
dally	jetty
dandy	jerky
doubly	jockey
dreamy	jury
duly	justly
dusky	lily
duty	ruddy
empty	rudely
filly	saintly
gaily	saucy
gaudy	scurvy
ghastly	singly
glory	simply
gory	sleepy
greedy	snappy
grumpy	sorry
guilty	sunny

steady	injury	victory	credulity
strophe	infamy	villainy	curiosity
study	infancy	votary	customary
sweetly	infantry	watery	declivity
tally	jollity	wearily	deformity
tardy	knavery	wantonly	immaturity
thirsty	laity	womanly	immutability
trophy	laxity	worthily	impartiality
truly	legacy	absurdity	impecuniosity
trusty	leprosy	activity	impetuosity
twenty	lethargy	adversity	impiety
ugly	levity	affability	impossibility
vainly	liberty	affinity	importunity
vary	library	agility	impurity
wary	livery	alacity	inability
weary	lottery	allegory	inaccuracy
wealthy	loyalty	ambiguity	
whisky	lunacy	anatomy	incivility
worthy	majesty	animosity	inclemency
academy	malady	antiquity	incongruity
agony	melody	anxiety	inconsistency
amity	memory	apostasy	inconstanoy
anarchy	misery	apostrophe	indemnity
apathy	modesty	aristocracy	inequality
artery	monarchy	astronomy	infidelity
augury	mummery	austerity	infinity
battery	mutiny	authority	infirmary
beggary	mystery	auxiliary	inflexibility
bigamy	nicety	aviary	insanity
bigotry	noisily	brevity	instability
blasphemy	novelty	calamity	integrity
botany	nunnery	capacity	intensity
bravery	nursery	captivity	liberality
bribery	penalty	catastrophe	loquacity
brevity	penury	complexity	luminosity
calumny	perfidy	concavity	preliminary
haughtily	perjury	confederacy	priority
history	piety	conformity	probability
honesty	pillory	congruity	prodigality
idolatry	piracy	conspiracy	profanity
industry	pleurisy	cosmography	profundity

123

propensity	nobly	courtesy	prodigy
prosperity	noisy	cruelty	progeny
radically	orgie	daintily	prosody
rapidly	pamly	dairy	purity
rascality	palfrey	decency	quality
reality	paltry	destiny	quantity
reciprocity	party	diary	raillery
rotundity	parsley	dignity	rectory
rudimentary	pastry	drapery	regency
satiety	petty	drollery	remedy
security	pigmy	drudgery	ribaldry
seniority	poorly	ecstasy	rivalry
sensibility	portly	elegy	robbery
sensuality	posy	embassy	royalty
severity	pretty	enemy	salary
simplicity	princely	energy	sanctity
sincerity	proudly	equity	secrecy
sobriety	pulley	eulogy	simony
society	purely	euphony	slavery
solemnity	queenly	factory	sorcery
solidity	quickly	family	strawberry
soliloquy	racy	fallacy	subsidy
sovereignty	rally	fealty	surgery
sublimity	rarely	fecundity	symmetry
kindly	rosy	finery	sympathy
kingly	rocky	flattery	symphony
knightly	roughly	foolery	tapestry
lady	ruby	foolishly	tragedy
lastly	canopy	gaiety	treachery
lonely	cavalry	gallantry	treasury
lordly	charity	gallery	trinity
lovely	chastity	galaxy	trumpery
manly	chemistry	granary	tyranny
marry	chivalry	gravity	urgency
meanly	clemency	poesy	unity
merry	colony	poetry	usury
misty	comedy	policy	vacancy
mouldy	company	potency	vanity
nasty	constancy	poverty	verily
neatly	cosily	primary	democracy
nearly	contrary	privacy	discovery

CPSIA information can be obtained
at www.ICGtesting.com
Printed in the USA
BVOW06s0932231017
498232BV00023B/253/P